John
HERSEY
and
James
AGEE

a reference guide

A
Reference
Publication
in
Literature

Ronald Gottesman
Editor

John
HERSEY
and
James
AGEE

a reference guide

NANCY LYMAN HUSE

G.K.HALL&CO.

70 LINCOLN STREET, BOSTON, MASS.

Library of Congress Cataloging in Publication Data
Huse, Nancy Lyman.
   John Hersey and James Agee: a reference guide.

   (A Reference publication in literature)
Includes index.
   1. Hersey, John Richard, 1914-   — Bibliography.
2. Agee, James, 1909-1955 — Bibliography.   I. Title.
II. Series.
Z8400.3.H87   [PS3515.E7715]   016.813'5'209   78-15368
ISBN 0-8161-8019-9

This publication is printed on permanent/durable acid-free paper
MANUFACTURED IN THE UNITED STATES OF AMERICA

Contents

Writings by John Hersey

BOOKS

Men on Bataan. New York: Alfred A. Knopf, 1942.

Into the Valley. New York: Alfred A. Knopf, 1942. New York:
    Bantam, 1966.

A Bell for Adano. New York: Alfred A. Knopf, 1944. New York:
    Avon Books, 1956.

Hiroshima. New York: Alfred A. Knopf, 1946. New York: Bantam, 1966.

The Wall. New York: Alfred A. Knopf, 1950.

The Marmot Drive. New York: Alfred A. Knopf, 1953. New York:
    The Popular Library, 1960.

A Single Pebble. New York: Alfred A. Knopf, 1956. New York:
    Bantam, 1968.

The War Lover. New York: Alfred A. Knopf, 1959. New York: Bantam,
    1960.

The Child Buyer. New York: Alfred A. Knopf, 1960.

Here to Stay. New York: Alfred A. Knopf, 1963.

White Lotus. New York: Alfred A. Knopf, 1965. New York: Bantam,
    1967.

Too Far to Walk. New York: Alfred A. Knopf, 1966. New York:
    Bantam, 1967.

Under the Eye of the Storm. New York: Alfred A. Knopf, 1967.
    New York: Bantam, 1968.

The Algiers Motel Incident. New York: Alfred A. Knopf, 1968.

Letter to the Alumni. New York: Alfred A. Knopf, 1970. New York:
    Bantam, 1971.

The Conspiracy. New York: Alfred A. Knopf, 1972.

My Petition for More Space. New York: Alfred A. Knopf, 1974.

The Writer's Craft. New York: Alfred A. Knopf, 1974.

The President. New York: Alfred A. Knopf, 1975.

The Walnut Door. New York: Alfred A. Knopf, 1977.

SELECTED ARTICLES AND SHORT STORIES

"Alternatives to Apathy." United Nations World (May, 1947), pp. 20, 21, 75, 76.

"The Death of Buchan Walsh." The Atlantic Monthly (April, 1946), pp. 80-86.

"Dialogue on Gorki Street." Fortune (January, 1945), pp. 149-51.

"Engineers of the Soul." Time (October 9, 1944), pp. 99-102.

"A Fable South of Cancer." '47, Magazine of the Year (April, 1947), pp. 113-41.

"Kamikaze." Life (July 3, 1944), pp. 68-75.

"Letter from Chungking." The New Yorker (March 16, 1946), pp. 80-87.

"Letter from Shanghai." The New Yorker (February 9, 1946), pp. 74-82.

"The Life of the Word." Images, Arlington Heights, Illinois: John Hersey High School, 1969, p. 1.

"The Mechanics of a Novel." The Yale University Library Gazette, 27 (July, 1952), pp. 1-11.

"The Novel of Contemporary History." The Atlantic Monthly (November, 1949), pp. 80-84.

"The One Without Whom...." Yale Daily News (January 18, 1967).

"The Pen." The Atlantic Monthly (June, 1946), pp. 84-87.

"A Reporter in China." The New Yorker (May 18, 1946), pp. 59-69; (May 25, 1946), pp. 54-69.

"A Short Wait." The New Yorker (June 14, 1947), pp. 27-29.

"Why Were You Sent Out Here?" The Atlantic Monthly (February, 1947), pp. 88-91.

Writings by James Agee

Permit Me Voyage. New Haven: Yale University Press, 1934.

Let Us Now Praise Famous Men. Boston: Houghton Mifflin, 1941.

The Morning Watch. Boston: Houghton Mifflin, 1951.

A Death in the Family. New York: McDowell, Obolensky, 1957.

Agee on Film: Reviews and Comments. New York: McDowell, Obolensky, 1958.

Agee on Film, Vol. II: Five Film Scripts. New York: McDowell, Obolensky, 1960.

Let Us Now Praise Famous Men. 2nd ed., includes foreword by Walker Evans. Boston: Houghton Mifflin, 1960.

The Letters of James Agee to Father Flye. Edited by James H. Flye. New York: George Braziller, 1962.

Four Early Stories by James Agee. Collected by Elena Harap. West Branch, Iowa: The Cummington Press, 1964.

The Collected Short Prose of James Agee. Edited, and with "A Memoir" by Robert Fitzgerald. Boston: Houghton Mifflin, 1968.

The Collected Poems of James Agee. Edited, and with introduction, by Robert Fitzgerald. Boston: Houghton Mifflin, 1968.

A Way of Seeing. (Introduction for a book of photographs by Helen Levitt.) New York: Viking, 1965.

The Letters of James Agee to Father Flye. 2nd ed., includes letters of Flye to Agee. Boston: Houghton Mifflin, 1971.

JOHN HERSEY
(1914-   )

Introduction

John Hersey, the son of Roscoe and Grace Baird Hersey, was born
in Tientsin, China, where his parents were missionaries. Until he
was ten, Hersey attended British and American schools in Tientsin.
After his family's return to the United States in 1924, he attended
public schools in Briarcliff Manor, New York, before entering Hotchkiss
and Yale, where he majored in History, Arts and Letters. As a Mellon
Fellow at Clare College, Cambridge, he studied eighteenth-century English literature before deciding to leave the academic life to become
a writer.

After a summer as secretary to Sinclair Lewis, Hersey worked as a
reporter for Time, Life, and The New Yorker from 1939 until 1946.
While serving as a war correspondent first in the Pacific and later
in Europe, he published four books: Men on Bataan (1942); Into the
Valley (1943); A Bell for Adano (1944); and Hiroshima (1946). A
Pulitzer Prize for A Bell for Adano and acclaim for the New Yorker
essay Hiroshima apparently influenced Hersey to become what he has
termed "a novelist of contemporary history." Following publication
of The Wall (1950), a dramatic chronicle about the Warsaw ghetto, he
settled in Connecticut and devoted most of his energy to writing fiction, usually of a topical nature and with a contemporary setting.

The War Lover (1959) examines the motivation of aviators during
World War II; White Lotus (1965) is an allegory about race relations
in the United States; eight additional novels deal with such topics
as education, modern anomie, and overpopulation. In addition to his
prolific output of fiction, Hersey has published several pieces of
journalism such as The Algiers Motel Incident (1968), which was the
result of his personal conviction that police brutality had occurred
in a Detroit shoot-out with young blacks; and The President (1975), a
series of interviews with Gerald Ford similar to those he had con-
ducted with Harry Truman for Life three decades earlier.

Hersey's concern with contemporary history is reflected in his
politically active life. In 1953 he campaigned for Adlai Stevenson
and drafted many of the candidate's speeches. He has been a member
of the Authors' Guild, where one of his projects has been the passage
of protective copyright legislation. He has also taken a number of

controversial stands on political questions, including his insistence on reading from Hiroshima at the White House Festival of Arts in protest against the Johnson administration's escalation of the Vietnam War. Long before the Watergate era, Hersey worked with The Committee to End Government Secrecy, a group of intellectuals who are interested in examining the roles of the F.B.I. and the C.I.A. In 1965, Hersey began to teach creative writing at Yale. It is his policy to avoid media exposure, but he occasionally speaks in public and has granted interviews and corresponded with students of his work.

When I asked Hersey, during an interview at his home in New Haven in 1973, to name the writers of his generation he most respects, he cited Lillian Hellman, Robert Penn Warren, and Arthur Miller. Significantly, these writers share to some degree the themes and reputation that have marked Hersey's development as a writer. They are, like Sinclair Lewis, issue-oriented writers, well known but not necessarily well received by critics. Though Hersey's early books generated many magazine and book reviews, most of his work since White Lotus (1965) has been quietly received.

During the war years, reviewers praised what they saw as historical accuracy and moral consciousness, though comments from such critics as Diana Trilling (1944.B10) and David Daiches (1950.B5) are typical of two strains in Hersey reviews throughout his career. Trilling condemned what she labeled a "contrived simplicity" in A Bell for Adano, while Daiches's sympathetic review of The Wall placed it outside the realm of great literature despite its splendid moral sense and complex characterization. Daiches felt that Hersey's use of actual events and of survivors' accounts removed the work from the genre of fiction and placed it in a category which could not be evaluated by the standards of the modern novel. Like the majority of Hersey's reviewers, Daiches praised the craftsmanship and story-telling gift of the writer. A number of commentators, including Howard Mumford Jones, Maxwell Geismar, Alfred Kazin and Edward Weeks followed Hersey's career with a nurturing interest, impressed with his skills but, as in the case of Geismar's review of The Wall, urging him to depict the dark side of human motivation. Kazin's (1971.B1) final classification of Hiroshima as a moral failure is related to the same view Daiches had in evaluating The Wall; Hersey's use of actual, catastrophic events removes him from the stream of modern psychological and symbolic novelists. In addition, Hersey's implicit belief that human beings can make order out of chaos has provoked comments by Leslie Fiedler, Kingsley Widmer and Warren French that echo Diana Trilling's dismissal of Hersey as simplistic. The combination of his journalistic forms and crusading tone overwhelmed these critics, who have found Hersey an example of the mediocrity of popular culture.

Just as media reviewers began to pay less attention to Hersey's new books, academic critics began to suggest that Hersey's work is valuable enough to be examined from a variety of perspectives.

Introduction to John Hersey

In 1966, David Sanders urged that he be classified as "a writer," so that comparisons with experimental novelists could be avoided. In his Twayne series volume (1967.A1) Sanders identified survival as Hersey's major theme and contended that he had been shut out of academic criticism because he constantly changed generic patterns and-- due to Hersey's unusual childhood and wide travel--changed subject matter as well, thus constituting too great a critical challenge for most students of literature. In 1969, Robert M. Hudspeth argued that Hersey's The War Lover effectively dramatized modern nihilism as defined by Hannah Arendt and other humanistic philosophers. This article and others, together with Sanders's book, marked the first time that serious critics found Hersey's work more than stylistically excellent or morally admirable. A real coherence of form, content, and intention was now being perceived.

In 1972, Samuel Girgus wrote an American Studies dissertation (University of New Mexico) arguing that Hersey's complex synthesis of contemporary thought challenges popular assumptions despite its affirmative interpretation of human experience. Michael Haltresht (1973.B1) analyzed White Lotus as Hersey's mythic response to the tragedy of The Wall; the collective ego--dreams, stories, and memory-- of the oppressed race allowed it to triumph instead of enduring the defeat suffered by the ghetto inhabitants. In 1975, my dissertation under John G. Cawelti at Chicago examined the background, rhetorical intention, and structuring principle of Hersey's work. Arguing that approaches relying mainly on the tenets of New Criticism needed balancing by generic and historical criteria, I described Hersey as one of those writers such as H. G. Wells and Sinclair Lewis whose rhetoric is central to a consistent and valid philosophy of life and art. Hersey's work goes beyond the theme of survival to what might be called a language act designed to ensure humanistic reshaping of the world.

Recent critical theorists have recognized that direct interpolation of writers' views is not a weakness per se. For example, Frank Kermode has favorably reassessed Arnold Bennett, Wayne Booth has analyzed the rhetoric of fiction, and William Stott's analysis of the documentary (focusing on Agee but drawing on interviews with Hersey and a number of others), suggests the evolution of criteria suited to most of Hersey's best work.

In preparing this bibliography, I was as inclusive as I could be without being repetitive. The early years generated many reviews, the later ones few--and this is reflected in the number of annotations for each book. I excluded reviews which merely summarized. To my knowledge, all academic criticism of Hersey's work is included.

I am indebted to the research librarians at Augustana College (Illinois), especially Mary Joyce Pickett and Martha Harris, for their good-natured and skillful help in locating materials. The Faculty Research Committee at Augustana assisted with a grant to cover expenses. Linda Biggiam expertly typed the manuscript.

Writings about John Hersey (1942-1977)

1942 A BOOKS - NONE

1942 B SHORTER WRITINGS

1   ANON. Review of <u>Men on Bataan</u>. <u>Time</u>, 39 (June 1), 80.
    Hersey demonstrates the presence of heroes in the war by
    structuring his account into two books about different kinds
    of heroic figures. The story of MacArthur is written in a
    shrewd and competent manner suited to the subject, while
    the story of the fighting men reproduces their courage and
    honor in the unforced flow of feelings and words typical of
    the best music and writing.

2   FADIMAN, CLIFTON. Review of <u>Men on Bataan</u>. <u>The New Yorker</u>,
    18 (June 6), 78.
    Declares that the facts about Bataan are in themselves
    a form of heroic poetry. Hersey succeeds, despite his use
    of <u>Timestyle</u>, in creating living men out of the soldiers he
    observed. MacArthur is depicted as a figure of great vigor,
    intelligence and military genius--but probably limited out-
    side of his own field.

3   MILLIS, WALTER. "The Superb Drama of MacArthur and His Men."
    <u>New York Herald Tribune Books</u> (May 31), p. 3.
    Through an unusual, somewhat distracting, but finally
    effective method, Hersey succeeds in telling the tragic
    story of Bataan. With balance and judgment, he relates both
    the biography and an analysis of MacArthur. The great
    strength of the leaders, fighters, and citizens points to
    the success which must come after these trials.

4   PRATT, FLETCHER. "The Epic of Bataan." <u>Saturday Review</u>, 25
    (June 4), 20.
    The war is finally producing literature which will be
    read without shame long after the battle is over. <u>Men on
    Bataan</u> goes beyond good reporting to a new combination of
    good journalism and personal experience. The thematic
    motif of the failure of democracy is juxtaposed subtly

1942

with its success in the form of events and conversations that convey hope for the future. The book ought to be read by every participant in the war; it comes terribly late, but not irrevocably so.

5   WILLIAMSON, S. T. Review of <u>Men on Bataan</u>. <u>New York Times</u> (June 6), p. 4.
        Hersey has made the best possible use of the resources currently available on his subject. Later books may include more data, but they probably will not surpass Hersey's craftsmanship and dramatic power.

1943 A BOOKS - NONE

1943 B SHORTER WRITINGS

1   ADAMS, J. DONALD. "New Books in Review." <u>Yale Review</u>, 32 (Summer), 791.
        In a review of <u>Into the Valley</u>, Adams states that it is one of a group of war books which show greater quality than those produced during the First World War. The war correspondents seem to have the awareness and perception needed by the statesmen, the civil servants, and the military. In his brief narrative, Hersey chooses one "unforgettably right detail" after another. His book recalls <u>The Red Badge of Courage</u>.

2   ANON. Review of <u>Into the Valley</u>. <u>Atlantic</u>, 171 (May), 123.
        The terse, beautifully written account of men in battle pays tribute to heroes and keeps the writer himself suitably in the background. The word choice demonstrates Hersey's accurate ear for dialogue.

3   ANON. Review of <u>Into the Valley</u>. <u>Catholic World</u>, 157 (August), 558.
        This compact, realistic war report offers readers the opportunity to know firsthand what war is like in a bloody, humid jungle.

4   ANON. Review of <u>Into the Valley</u>. <u>Time</u>, 41 (February 8), 91.
        Hersey gives an unpretentious account of three days in battle. The reviewer quotes extensively from the book in order to demonstrate Hersey's effectiveness as a writer.

5   ANON. "News of the Week." <u>Publishers Weekly</u>, 143 (March 20), 1277.

Since Into the Valley was named "Imperative reading" by
the Council on Books in Wartime, 6,000 copies have been
sold. Knopf is advertising it with 400-line ads, and other
publishers are including it in their ads. Posters have
been placed in libraries and bookstores, and Hersey has
been on the radio to discuss his experience.

6   BRANT, IRVING. Review of Into the Valley. New Republic, 108
    (March 1), 292.
       This book will become part of readers' permanent collec-
    tions, and will be an enduring contribution to the litera-
    ture of World War II. It is written with the "art that
    conceals art," such as the subtle device Hersey used in
    relating the story of Rigaud's boyhood to create a sense
    of impending tragedy.

7   CHAMBERLAIN, JOHN. "Readers and Writers in War Time." Yale
    Review, 33 (September), 1-13.
       War books have an unfortunate tendency to present a
    single "keep fighting" tone, and Hersey's Into the Valley
    is no exception. His book does, however, have something to
    say about American culture. He learned first-hand that
    democracy cultivates adaptability and self-reliance, yet is
    flexible enough to provide for voluntary group action when
    it is needed. Americans are repeatedly taught they cannot
    and must not fail.

8   GOETTE, JOHN. "The Shadow of the Valley." Saturday Review,
    26 (February 13), 10.
       Into the Valley does not proselytize for any belief ex-
    cept confidence that American fighters can perform the hor-
    rendous tasks required by war because of their love for
    their homes and families. Hersey has produced one of the
    good pieces of writing from this conflict, using repetition
    as a careful literary device. Read at one sitting, the book
    causes the reader to experience the suffering and spirit of
    the men on Guadalcanal.

9   O'NEIL, WILL. Review of Into the Valley. The Chicago Sun
    (March 21), p. 1.
       Hersey's account is a record of action rather than of
    thought. It allows the reader to experience vicariously
    the ordeal of the men battling in the jungle.

10 WILLIAMSON, S. T. Review of Into the Valley. New York Times
    (February 7), p. 4.
       Hersey's simply told story reveals a great deal about
    the mysterious and unpleasant psychology of war. It is not
    unreasonable to rank it beside Crane's Red Badge of Courage.

1944

1944 A BOOKS - NONE

1944 B SHORTER WRITINGS

1   ANON. Review of A Bell for Adano. Kirkus, 12 (January 15), 21.
        This story is causing much debate, because it allegedly presents a dramatization of an incident from General Patton's career which had best be forgotten. Attention should be given instead to the sensitive picture of democracy supplanting facism.

2   ANON. "After Victory." Time, 43 (February 21), 99.
        A Bell for Adano is a first novel comprised of sharp war reporting and self-consciously hard-boiled fiction. The bitter mood alternates with a wild, raucous humor, yielding a powerful impact resembling a kick from one of the mules on the road to Adano. Both the villain and the hero are presented without shadings. Despite the critical attitude toward the incompatibility of U.S. military officials, the tone of the book is that the war was essentially a battle to preserve democracy.

3   ANON. "Reason vs. Officialdom." Christian Science Monitor (April 22), p. 10.
        A Bell for Adano offers an argument well suited to its novelistic form, the conflict that a reasonable and plain person would necessarily feel in carrying out the commands of unjust officials. Though the plot is slight, Hersey gives rich pictures of places and of people.

4   COWLEY, MALCOLM. "Novels after the War." New Republic, 110 (February 14), 216.
        Like Steinbeck and Hemingway, Hersey combines war observations with his literary memories. A Bell for Adano is entertaining and effective as a tract, and it should not be expected to meet the criteria for the novel as well.

5   HINDUS, MILTON. Review of A Bell for Adano. Atlantic, 173 (March), 131.
        A Bell for Adano has merit as both a novel and a report. It suggests that government is only as good as the people who govern, with Joppolo offered as a symbol of what is best in the American character or even in all of humanity. Hersey's recurrent theme is individual worth, dramatized with his talent for concrete observation rather than theoretical ponderings.

6   PRESCOTT, ORVILLE. "Outstanding Novels." Yale Review, 33
    (Summer), 764-68.
         Responding to a Harper's article in which Diana Trilling
    had lamented the absence of creativity in current fiction
    (May, 1944), the reviewer suggests that Hersey's A Bell for
    Adano offers hope for American letters. It is the more re-
    markable in being written under wartime pressures.

7   REDMAN, BEN RAY. "A Man of Good Will." Saturday Review, 27
    (February 12), 8.
         A Bell for Adano surpasses the promise Hersey offered in
    his earlier books. Despite its subject, the novel is gay--
    yet it conveys a powerful message. It shows Hersey's many-
    sided talent, playing the range of humor from whimsey to
    farce and yet able to portray the sober and the serious.
    Plot construction is tight and admirable; characters are
    types, but superb examples of good and evil. The book
    states that the ultimate war aim of most men is to go home.

8   SAPIEHA, VIRGINIA. "With the Americans in a Sicilian Village."
    New York Herald Tribune Book Review (February 6), p. 1.
         A Bell for Adano underscores the traditional good will
    toward men which characterizes American occupation forces
    at their best. Hersey draws an important distinction be-
    tween the attitudes of the Italian peasants or "primitives,"
    and the American soldiers or "neo-primitives." American
    ideals of freedom and justice are implicit within the story.

9   SPECTORSKY, A. C. "American Men of AMGOT in Italy." Book
    Week (February 6), p. 1.
         Solid information and a portrait of a certain "General
    Marvin" make this book well worth time and money. Its
    story is enjoyable, but Hersey fails to understand the
    people he describes or to examine the implications of their
    actions.

10 TRILLING, DIANA. "Fiction in Review." Nation, 158
    (February 12), 194-95.
         When Hersey wrote A Bell for Adano, he worked quickly
    and drew from folk idealism and popular assumptions. There
    is a good deal of apparent truth in his contrived simplic-
    ity; Joppolo is a compendium of the idealized national
    character. The book is disappointing in that Hersey knows
    better; he could have avoided the exaggeration and falsify-
    ing that go into a popular book, and told the truth about
    the war as a reporter and an artist.

1944

11   WEEKS, EDWARD. Review of <u>A Bell for Adano</u>. <u>Atlantic</u>, 173
     (April), 127.
         <u>A Bell for Adano</u> is a morality tale with oversimplified
     characters to make points about the battle between good and
     evil. Hersey is especially effective in capturing the char-
     acter of the common people, of lower ranking officers and
     citizens, who reveal both human strength and weakness.
     Their reactions to the blind warfare machine can remind
     readers of the difficulties to be faced in the immediate
     future.

1946 A BOOKS - NONE

1946 B SHORTER WRITINGS

1   ANON. "Talk of the Town." <u>Newsweek</u>, 28 (September 9), 69-71.
         In printing "Hiroshima" as one issue of their magazine,
     <u>New Yorker</u> editors showed their independence from reader
     expectation. After William Shawn conceived the idea, Hersey
     had to rewrite the article under the pressures of time and
     secrecy. The article has met a fantastic reception, in-
     cluding the purchase of 1,000 copies by Albert Einstein.
     Hersey is insisting on wide distribution, but will not allow
     the essay to be dramatized in film or theater.

2   ANON. Review of <u>Hiroshima</u>. <u>Kirkus</u>, 114 (September 15), 471.
         This book is an artistic achievement, notable for its
     classic restraint and simplicity, its implicit severity.
     It cannot fail to move its readers. Hersey has risen to
     the heights of his profession, transforming impartial re-
     cording into a strong, human document.

3   ANON. "Hiroshima." <u>Christian Century</u>, 63 (September),
     1143-44.
         John Hersey's <u>New Yorker</u> article on the effects of our
     bombing Hiroshima offers a truth never found in statistics,
     the human dimension available only through the imagination.
     Without preaching, Hersey creates six characters who cannot
     fail to have an impact on readers. There is some distortion
     of the war, since nothing is said about the slaughter in the
     rest of the world, but this is not a defect of the method;
     it is necessary to focus solely on the effects of this new
     weapon. The acute suffering of the victims raises an im-
     portant question about modern warfare: what ethical posi-
     tion must we hold concerning the bombing of civilians?
     They are, after all, the suppliers of the armed forces--yet
     the force of this bomb implies that from now on all people

1946

are potentially victims when a nation goes to war. It is crucial that World War III never occur.

4 ANON. Review of Hiroshima. Times Literary Supplement (London) (December 7), p. 605.
Hersey's decision to let the facts of the disaster speak for themselves results in an account that is too quiet. Using survivors as narrators puts the dead into the background, further weakening the piece.

5 BENEDICT, RUTH. "The Past and the Future." Nation, 163 (December 7), 656.
Hiroshima requires its readers to make value judgments about the atomic bomb, even though it contains no direct preaching. Another significant aspect of the work is that it is a sourcebook for Japanese behavior. The populace did not attack the Westerners present, nor was there mass hysteria. The silence, and the tendency to assist relatives and friends rather than to organize massive rescue attempts, suggest a philosophic stand basic to the culture. It is desirable to control one's own pain, preserving self-respect by observing the amenities.

6 BLIVEN, BRUCE. Review of Hiroshima. New Republic, 115 (September 9), 300.
Hersey's report will certainly become a great classic of the war. It unquestionably deserves the Pulitzer Prize for journalism.

7 HIRSCH, RUDOLPH. Review of Hiroshima. Library Journal, 71 (November), 1539.
Hersey's essay on the bombing of Hiroshima gives an unpleasant but instructive and thought-provoking dramatization of a major issue of World War II. His writing forces the reader to assess his values and take a stand.

8 HUTCHISON, RUSSELL S. Review of "Hiroshima." Christian Century, 63 (September 25), 1151.
In an act of rare discernment, Hersey has looked deeply into the American conscience, and without preaching has created a factual moral exposition. Reasons to read his New Yorker essay include its presentation of facts, its description of Japanese life, its indirect questioning of ethics, and its miniature sketch of the horrors of future wars.

9 POORE, CHARLES. Review of Hiroshima. New York Times (November 10), p. 7.

1946

In book form, Hersey's account of the bombing will have
the potential of reaching all of us, and it should. The
book speaks for itself better than any commentary on it,
and in a way, it speaks for the entire human race.

10   RIDENAUR, LOUIS. Review of Hiroshima. Saturday Review, 29
(November 2), 16.
The clear, objective report on Hiroshima forces the
reader to consider and decide moral questions at once. The
book should be read by every literate person, and then all
of us should begin discussions about its implications for
our lives as moral beings.

1950 A BOOKS - NONE

1950 B SHORTER WRITINGS

1   ANGOFF, CHARLES. "John Hersey's Ghetto." American Mercury
(May), pp. 623-31.
It is too soon to deal with Nazi terror in literature;
we need "a prolonged brooding period." Though Hersey's
interest in separate Jews as people and his profound sympathy and admiration for them is clear, the diary form of
his book obscures his tremendous subject and prevents the
reader from becoming immersed in the material. Not all of
the history is accurate; most of the ghetto inhabitants were
poor and orthodox rather than the middle class intellectuals
Hersey depicts. Socialism was integral to Zionism, yet
hardly figures in the book. Characterization is flat; even
Levinson remains a "shadowy figure."

2   ANON. Review of The Wall. Time, 55 (March 6), 96.
Hersey's attempt to write fiction instead of journalism
is a failure. Noach Levinson is too introspective and intellectual to do the work assigned to him. The use of the
diary is one of the oldest and least effective of technical
tricks.

3   COGLEY, JOHN. "There Remain These Three." Commonweal, 51
(March 17), 608-10.
Hersey is a writer of magnificent talents. Anyone who
wants to write about modern history is compelled to write
about individual men and women. It is shameful that apathy
permitted the holocaust; the entire debacle evoked less out-
cry from American Catholics than has been expressed over one
obscene novel. Out of the horror, Hersey creates marvelous
human beings like Levinson and Rachel Apt. He brilliantly

14

conveys to the reader the experience of a faith and a culture not his own. It shows him to be a first-rate craftsman
and outstanding human being who arouses in others the virtues of faith, hope, and charity.

4   COUSINS, NORMAN. "John Hersey." <u>Saturday Review</u>, 33
    (March 4), 15.
       Hersey is convinced that human emotions and values are
    the basis of writing about even the most cataclysmic event.
    He has a profound sense of purpose when he writes, devoting
    the most careful research to his history-in-the-making.
    <u>The Wall</u> will contribute to American literature as well as
    to Hersey's reputation.

5   DAICHES, DAVID. "Record and Testament." <u>Commentary</u> (April),
    pp. 385-88.
       Asserts that <u>The Wall</u> book cannot be read or discussed
    purely as a fiction. Our knowledge that the massacre was
    real is part of our reading experience. The events are not
    symbolic; they are actual. Hersey gives us "the record of
    his own noble and almost desperate sympathy." Through
    Levinson, Hersey conducts a search for the victims and for
    the meaning of their slaughter. Despite flaws in the style
    of the diary, the book's structure achieves significance by
    virtue of the assiduous search. The detailed progression
    of the diary shows the slow disintegration of the ghetto
    populace. It also depicts the constant efforts to sustain
    life which helped to prolong the disintegration.
       The book rests on no thesis about the meaning of the
    Warsaw massacre, but raises an important question. How
    should the persecuted minority, which is made up of people
    from diverse backgrounds, respond to the world? The unity
    and resistance suggested by the novel provide only temporary
    responses. The answer offered by Levinson through Peretz,
    cultural cross-fertilization, does not answer the practical
    questions it brings with it. Hersey suggests that the real
    strength must come from within the Jewish community; only
    then will respect engender a reciprocal humanism in the
    larger society.
       Hersey's writing has the quality of astringency in this
    novel because he is not afraid to reveal weaknesses in his
    characters. His work answers one question; he shows what
    ought to be the attitude of the civilized and humane non-
    Jew to the horror. The few factual errors are offset by
    the generally accurate historical background. Whatever
    else the book may be, it will continue a remarkable testa-
    ment to Hersey's own consciousness.

1950

6   GEISMAR, MAXWELL. "The Wall." Saturday Review, 33 (March 4), 14-16.
    Reviewing The Wall, Geismar states that Hersey has combined daily life, history, and social analysis through an "inner exposition." The book lacks a final sense of horror and evil, taking a tone that is too delicate for the content. It is, however, "an urgent and remarkable novel on a grand scale." Reprinted, with commentary: 1958.B2.

7   GREENBERG, ELIEZER. "The Mark of Cain." Nation, 170 (March 11), 231.
    States that Hersey gives a strong, bitter testimony to the six million innocent dead of the holocaust. The Wall is rich in detail, sympathy, patience, and research. It operates on only one level of tragedy, failing to gather strength through rhythm and mood and thus lacking in prophetic insight. It is, however, accurate history and writing that will burn "the mark of Cain on man's consciousness."

8   GUILFOIL, KELSEY. "John Hersey: Fact and Fiction." English Journal, 39 (September), 355-60.
    The "journalism" label attributed to Hersey implies that his work is lacking in depth and in the power to build reader identification. This does not quite do justice to Hersey, since the label does not reflect the honesty of purpose and clarity of view he brings to his material. He is remarkable for his integrity and accuracy, and Hiroshima puts him in a high place among living writers. His status as a novelist cannot yet be determined.

9   HATCH, ROBERT. "The Man Who Attends Catastrophes." New Republic, 122 (April 3), 18.
    The Wall is an admirable journalistic narrative, but it is not possible to call it a great novel. Hersey attends catastrophes to observe people enduring extreme situations. He has become "a witness for humanity in a time of terror," one who finds out precisely what happened and conveys the information in a way that engages the reader in a bond of respect and allegiance. This limits his creativity, since he imposes plot on character and does not infuse the facts with his own spirit. In The Wall, he uses to advantage his facility for detail and builds an elaborate, complex pattern. Levinson himself is a superb journalist whom only Hersey could create. His account of the events is both inspiring and unforgettable.

10   JACKSON, JOSEPH. "A Memorable Novel on the Warsaw Ghetto." San Francisco Chronicle (February 26), p. 14.

"Great" is not too big a word to say of The Wall.
Hersey avoids telling just a tale of noble resistance, and
instead creates a universal work mirroring the complexity
of life through the history of the Warsaw ghetto.

11 KALEM, THEODORE. "Morally Honorable, Deeply Humane."
    Christian Science Monitor (March 11), p. 5.
       In The Wall, Hersey achieves a conscious blending of
    research, report, mimetics, and sympathy. Though he has
    erred in letting facts speak for themselves in some places,
    the cumulative effect of the book is an eloquent prod to
    readers' consciences. The novel is more aptly described as
    moral fervor than as literature. The characters might be
    our next-door neighbors; their culture is skin-deep.

12 KAZIN, ALFRED. "John Hersey and Noach Levinson." New Yorker,
    26 (March 4), 96-100.
       Though The Wall does not equal the depth of the survi-
    vors' own accounts, it is a remarkable, touching book which
    offers sympathy and love in the face of the holocaust. It
    is a model of a bridge between cultures, an "imaginative
    act of human solidarity." It helps to alleviate some of
    the bitterness Jews have felt over the gentile distance
    from events. This quality of interchange saves the book
    from its weaknesses, which include touches of inaccuracy,
    and, more seriously, a failure to realize the implications
    of his subject for government, politics, and history.
       Hersey does not link the horror with the prevalent moral
    attitude which sees man as the helpless victim of events.
    He concentrates on the dignity of individuals such as
    Levinson, creating a human genius superior to any character-
    ization by more successful political writers like Orwell and
    Koestler. Both Hersey and his diarist have "the great
    human gift for entering into a world not immediately our
    own."

13 PICKREL, PAUL. "Outstanding Novels." Yale Review, 39
    (Spring), 573.
       States that The Wall is a powerful answer to the follow-
    ing question: "'What can life mean when war, pestilence,
    starvation, and every kind of brutality and violence known
    to man become its everyday conditions?'" Hersey's choice
    of subject explains much; he combines a strong feeling for
    tradition with equally strong liberal convictions, and sees
    people as part of a historic continuity, with the freedom
    to discover facts and to effect change. The reportorial
    structure is effective for this purpose, but it imposes some
    limitations on Levinson's characterization. The Wall is a

1950

tribute to a great occasion, not a great novel, but it differs from other political novels in allowing people, as
well as ideas, to live in the reader's consciousness.

14   REYNOLDS, QUENTIN. "Doomed People Who Refused to Die." New
York Times Book Review (February 26), 1.
The Wall tells a tragic story filled with heroism and
hope, and showing a grasp of life in a world of death. It
affirms our spiritual resources against the threat of over-
powering evil. Only a true and sensitive novelist could
have read and dramatized history in this way.

15   SHIRER, WILLIAM. "John Hersey's Superb Novel of the Agony of
Warsaw." New York Herald Tribune Book Review (February 26),
1.
The Wall is an impressive epic of the Jews and of all
men facing death. With it, Hersey almost leaps overnight
into the ranks of Wolfe, Dreiser, and Flaubert. He is
unique among serious American writers in his moral stance.
This tale of death suggests what life is actually about.

16   SULLIVAN, RICHARD. Review of The Wall. Chicago Sunday
Tribune (February 26), p. 3.
The critic's opinion changed as he read the book, because he realized that Hersey's method, like "frosted glass,"
permitted a detailed yet broad reconstruction of the horror
in Warsaw. The book is gripping, has complete integrity,
and should be read by a million people.

17   WEEKS, EDWARD. Review of The Wall. Atlantic, 185 (March),
72.
Hersey has done for the forties what Steinbeck did for
the thirties in his The Grapes of Wrath and In Dubious Bat-
tle. His fiction and reporting have conveyed both violent
experience and a moral reaction to it. With The Wall, he
has enlarged the documentary novel. His complicated structure and the filter of the diarist are effective in convey-
ing both scope and detail. "It is a story of humanity
transcending horror."

1952 A BOOKS - NONE

1952 B SHORTER WRITINGS

1   HEALY, ROBERT C. "Novelists of the War: A Bunch of Dispos-
sessed," in Fifty Years of the American Novel 1900-1950.
Edited by Harold C. Gardiner, S.J. New York: Scribner,
pp. 258-270.

The Wall was the "most distinguished novel inspired by
World War II" and the only one not related to the author's
own experience--something it has in common with War and
Peace and The Red Badge of Courage. The book affects all
people because it explores the heart and soul of humanity
in the tragic setting, giving a potent illusion of actual
truth. It bears no political message and argues no thesis
except that human dignity does exist. Hersey's conception
of life is directly opposite to Mailer's. These two writers
represent the tug-of-war going on in both American life and
American literature.

1953 A BOOKS - NONE

1953 B SHORTER WRITINGS

1   ANON. Review of The Marmot Drive. Kirkus, 21 (September 1),
     591.
         Hersey cannot be pigeonholed; his new book is totally
     different from preceding ones, yet succeeds completely in
     creating its own illusion. The story has an underlying
     bitterness, and is best described as a modern prose Spoon
     River Anthology.

2   ANON. Review of The Marmot Drive. Time, 62 (November 9),
     118.
         Hersey follows the convention of the novel which puts
     people into close quarters, and demonstrates their best and
     worst qualities. In this novel, smoky symbolism is the
     chief effect.

3   GEISMAR, MAXWELL. "The Crazy Mask of Literature." Nation,
     177 (November 14), 404.
         Asserts that The Marmot Drive is almost entirely an
     exercise in the darker side of consciousness, the area
     Geismar had asked Hersey to explore when he reviewed The
     Wall. Hersey does a creditable job in revealing personal
     frustration and mass cruelty in an idyllic setting. With
     its thin characterization, the book seems to be almost a
     parable or warning rather than a novel.

4   HOWE, IRVING. "Symbolic Suburbia." New Republic, 129
     (November 16), 17.
         In The Marmot Drive, Hersey has succumbed to Rich Prose
     and Symbolism. The style is annoyingly poetic, as well as
     "clever, caustic, contemplative, and philosophical." The
     work is not political commentary; Matthew is punished for

1953

his private flaw, not for his public mistakes. The exter-
nal surface of the book is flimsy and boring, so there is
nothing beneath it either. Major characters are streams
of anxieties, while minor characters are ferociously eccentric. Both are irrelevant.

5   JACKSON, JOSEPH. "The New John Hersey." San Francisco
     Chronicle (November 12), p. 17.
         The Marmot Drive contains murky symbolism, but Hersey
     does achieve depth of characterization in this strange tale.
     Echoes of Shirley Jackson's "The Lottery" and of James Gould
     Cozzens's Dr. Adam seem to be present.

6   JONES, HOWARD MUMFORD. "New England Parable." Saturday
     Review, 36 (November 7), 22.
         States that The Marmot Drive differs from the intelligent
     sentimentalism of A Bell for Adano and the epic grandeur of
     The Wall. Instead, the book demands several readings, and
     its "pebbled, gnarled, knotted surface" is both admirable
     and puzzling. It is possible that the book is a failure on
     a very high plane; its meaning seems indecipherable. Yet
     it pulls one back to it.

7   RUGOFF, MILTON. "John Hersey's New Novel of Cross-Currents in
     a Yankee Town." New York Herald Tribune Book Review
     (November 8), p. 5.
         Hersey's The Marmot Drive is bizarre and fascinating,
     and possibly an experiment which went out of his control.
     It seems to be an attack on false values and also a drama-
     tization of the struggle between good and evil, but it is
     obscure. Like Into the Valley, this story is a stylistic-
     ally interesting quest-adventure, at least on one level.

1955 A BOOKS - NONE

1955 B SHORTER WRITINGS

1   FREDERICK, JOHN T. "Fiction of the Second World War."
     College English, 17 (January), 197-204.
         Groups Hersey's Into the Valley and Hiroshima with the
     work of other reporters such as Ernie Pyle, and states that
     they surpass all but a few of the novels about this war in
     their range, intensity and significance. Most fiction
     about this period is derivative of earlier writers, and
     fails to convey the meaning of the human struggle.

1956 A BOOKS - NONE

1956 B SHORTER WRITINGS

1   ARROWSMITH, WILLIAM. "More Bland than Mellow." New Republic,
     139 (August 13), 19.
         A Single Pebble fails to convey a sense of the tragic,
     foundering on the blandness in characterization, perception
     and ideas that is present. There is a well-shaped plot and
     some effective description, but throughout the book we re-
     spond more to Hersey's intent than to his accomplishment.
     The narrator has the vague, generous, optimistic and self-
     assured mind which lies behind a Life editorial. The death
     of Pebble seems to occur because the novel requires a death,
     and the engineer expresses elation at the moment of despair.
     Because Hersey is committed to a sense of dignity, he re-
     fuses to examine or to offend. The political is avoided
     entirely.

2   BROWN, ROBERT R. "Hersey and China." Christian Science
     Monitor (June 7), p. 7.
         In a review of A Single Pebble, the writer states that
     Hersey's sensitive, beautiful story leaves the reader to
     draw out the implicit lesson. The book shows a people in
     tune with the reality they have, imaged by the awesome
     river.

3   FIEDLER, LESLIE. "The Novel in the Post-Political World."
     Partisan Review, 23 (Summer), 358-65.
         A Single Pebble is one of four novels reviewed in this
     article. Fiedler states that Hersey surrenders imagination
     to sentimentality for the purpose of liberal moralizing.
     The novel is Hersey's way of self-servingly extolling the
     unrecognized virtues of failure, one more lament about the
     White Man's Burden. He must belittle himself in reparation
     for his role as oppressor in the past. Fiedler says, "...I
     find Hersey's sentiments so piously unexceptionable as to
     be intolerable." The book is not a novel, and Hersey is
     not a novelist. He uses fiction as a strategy for adver-
     tising his own point of view. The love story is a pretense
     at fiction; Hersey is lecturing.

4   GEISMAR, MAXWELL. "Against the Tide of Euphoria." Nation,
     182 (June 2), 473.
         Hersey's A Single Pebble provides a means of escape from
     the ordinary unthinking life. While his previous book, The
     Marmot Drive, was cold-blooded in its imaging of American
     fear and prejudice, this book is a seemingly delicate fable

1956

which is actually a dramatic, powerful drama of East and
West, and possibly Hersey's best work so far. The novel
recognizes the strength and beauty of a culture we are
taught is alien to ours.

5   HOGAN, WILLIAM. "John Hersey's Timeless Trip on the Yangtze."
San Francisco Chronicle (June 4), p. 23.
         A Single Pebble is a beautiful short novel which captures
in clear, lucid prose, reminiscent of Hersey's stylistic
materpiece Into the Valley, the essence of Chinese river
life. The plot concerns an American engineer who seems to
come under the spell of the river gods as he travels on the
Yangtze.

6   HORCHLER, R. T. "A Serious Fable." Commonweal, 64 (June 29),
329.
         In A Single Pebble, Hersey has moved from interest in
current events to interest in a mystical experience that
is quasi-religious. The tale succeeds on fundamental
lines, though the characterization is not wholly adequate.
The Chinese workers are depicted in a superficial manner,
and the narrator himself is merely a device for voicing the
author's rather vague ideas. The effect of the crisis on
the narrator is merely an ill-defined uplift--not a true
philosophical change.

7   HUGHES, RILEY. Review of A Single Pebble. Catholic World,
183 (July), 312.
         Hersey has produced an outstanding evocation of a magic
moment, dramatizing it almost flawlessly. A time past is
recaptured.

8   JONES, HOWARD MUMFORD. Review of A Single Pebble. Saturday
Review, 39 (June 2), 10.
         A Single Pebble is Hersey's recovery from the failure
of The Marmot Drive. It is the quality prose he has been
known for, a fable rather than a novella. A comparison to
The Old Man and the Sea is useful; the book is "a novel
whose dimensions are reduced without being truncated." This
sort of story requires a richness of texture and a depth in
time, space and experience--and Hersey does achieve these.
Style, not characterization, carries the theme. The journey
is depicted powerfully, but there are echoes of soap opera
after Pebble's death.

9   RUGOFF, MILTON. "John Hersey's Dramatic Tale of the Mighty
Yangtze." New York Herald Tribune Book Review (June 3),
p. 1.

22

In his novel of the Yangtze, Hersey returns to the level of his high stylistic and documentary achievements. Simple yet powerful, the novel has a care for detail and a thoroughly authentic tone. It is a very satisfying book.

10 WEEKS, EDWARD. "In the Gorge." Atlantic, 198 (August), 80.
A Single Pebble is a beautifully written novel which fulfills the promise Hersey showed in the war novels. It engenders a feeling of humility toward the East, but moves beyond topicality to creating a universal image of the person entering alien country convinced of possessing superior knowledge. Learning to depend on tradition, we appreciate virtues like tenacity and loyalty. The narrative propels the engineer to maturity as swiftly as the mythic river runs through the gorge.

1958 A BOOKS - NONE

1958 B SHORTER WRITINGS

1 FULLER, EDMUND J. Man in Modern Fiction. New York: Random House.
Mentions Hersey as the leader of a whole new generation of artists who "represent the affirmations or recognition of values in both familiar and new voices." Other writers in this group include Morton Thompson, James Agee, Brendan Gill, Gerald Green, J. F. Powers, Mary Renault, and Jan de Hartog. They are in the tradition of "believers," represented by such figures as Paul Tillich, Reinhold Niebuhr, C. S. Lewis, Alan Paton, Dorothy Sayers and others. These writers evaluate as well as record experience.

2 GEISMAR, MAXWELL. "John Hersey: The Revival of Conscience," in his American Moderns: From Rebellion to Conformity. New York: Hill and Wang, pp. 180-86.
States that his earlier review of The Wall (1950) was somewhat too fervent, but that he can still agree with it. The book is Hersey's best work to date, providing a good stage for his virtuosity and for his ability to deal with moral and social issues. It reminds one of earlier American novels dealing with such issues, which makes the work out of style. Critics equate social consciousness with Communism. Writers like Hersey take risks, and critics often refuse to join in the risks by praising a work which questions the established order.
But the Nazis' crimes were too terrible to be forgotten. They surpass even the horror of "the Bomb." Hersey's novel

1958

actually does not go far enough to depict the demonism of
the Germans. The emotional horror of the Warsaw ghetto is
not fully brought out. Hersey's next novel, The Marmot
Drive, may be an attempt to explore this horror because it
is a study of evil itself in terms of American society. It
is not fully successful because Hersey has difficulty por-
traying the darker side of reality. A Single Pebble is re-
stricted to the kind of emotional experience Hersey is
capable of dealing with, but it somehow is too fluid, too
beautiful to be taken seriously. Possibly Hersey "belongs
with those novelists of sensibility who are masters of
illusion, but not of life." He sees people in terms of a
situation or crisis. Our best writers have been able to
show the range and complexity of human emotion in and for
itself. Hersey needs more understanding of our motivations,
particularly of our "haunted unconscious." Nonetheless,
among our newer writers, Hersey deserves our esteem. Contains reprint of 1950.B6.

1959 A BOOKS - NONE

1959 B SHORTER WRITINGS

1   ANON. Review of The War Lover. Chicago Sunday Tribune
        (October 4), p. 3.
            Hersey shows superb insight, but uses too much detail
     in what could have been a great war novel. Perhaps Hersey's
     genius is for the short novel.

2   ANON. "In Love with Death." Time, 74 (October 5), 102.
            The War Lover, a thesis novel, is Hersey's most unsatis-
     factory piece of work so far. It lacks solid thought, re-
     sembling in its Freudian speculation the convictions of
     intellectuals in the thirties that wars could be blamed on
     a single cause, munitions manufacturers. As a reporter,
     however, Hersey excels in descriptive power.

3   BAILLIETT, WHITNEY. Review of The War Lover. The New Yorker,
        35 (December 19), 140.
            Hersey's story is really a detailed disguise for a
     sermon against war. At times, such as in the description
     of the flight back, he produces a remarkably sustained
     piece of creative literature. The book comes close to
     Hersey's dream of producing the great war novel of our
     time, but does not ultimately achieve the necessary
     greatness.

4   BOATWRIGHT, TALIAFERRO. "An Airman Who Gave His Soul to the
     God of Battle." New York Herald Tribune Book Review
     (October 4), p. 1.
         The War Lover is an exceptionally fine war novel, even
     though its philosophical assumptions may not be entirely
     tenable to the reader. Its characterization and narrative
     are superb. Daphne is certainly the best woman character
     in war fiction of the century.

5   HICKS, GRANVILLE. "John Hersey's Message." Saturday Review,
     42 (October 3), 59.
         As in The Wall, Hersey exhibits fine research skills in
     The War Lover. His method, however, deprives the reader of
     suspense, spoiling the book by telling all. Hersey is in
     deadly earnest, but his thesis that there is one all-
     encompassing cause for war is not intellectually tenable.
     His strengths as a reporter and his literary competence are
     undeniable, but do not result in greatness.

6   HOGAN, WILLIAM. "John Hersey's Novel of Wartime Flyers."
     San Francisco Chronicle (October 5), p. 37.
         Though The War Lover has a setting entirely different
     from Hersey's other novels, he has once again achieved ex-
     cellence in his craft. Using a form of documentary exact-
     ness to tell a psychological story, Hersey attacks those
     who engage in war for the pleasure of destructiveness.
     The Wall may be Hersey's finest novel, but The War Lover
     is a first-rate story that only Hersey could produce.

7   MAGID, NORA. Review of The War Lover. Commonweal, 71
     (November 27), 268.
         Comparing The War Lover to A Bell for Adano, the writer
     states that Hersey still falls into sentimentalism and
     manipulative style, but in this new book he also shows
     true emotion and a forthright picture of authority, aggres-
     sion, love, and loneliness. With its more controlled nar-
     rative and simple fabular quality, A Bell for Adano had its
     own strength. The newer novel is brilliant journalism and
     eminently moral, albeit lacking in humor.

8   MIZENER, ARTHUR. Review of The War Lover. New York Times
     (October 4), p. 1.
         Hersey has written a fine story, but marred it with his
     heavy-handed attempt to impose a generalized meaning on the
     acts of particular men. He can represent the surface of
     experience, but is inept when he probes its meaning.

1959

9   MURCHLAND, BERNARD. Review of The War Lover. Commonweal, 71
    (December 4), 297.
        Hersey succeeds in linking artistically two major
    maladies: war and neurosis. Though he has problems with
    characterization, Hersey's performance is masterful.

10 NORDELL, ROD. "A Novel of Fighting and Things Fought For."
    Christian Science Monitor (October 8), p. 15.
        The War Lover conveys a moral intention and theme despite
    its somewhat offensive surface, differing significantly and
    positively from other war novels of our era. It offers an
    object lesson about the causes of war as contemplated by
    the Everyman-narrator. Though heavy-handed in conveying
    his philosophy, Hersey is a master of realistic description.

11 RICHARDSON, MAURICE. Review of The War Lover. New Statesman,
    58 (October 31), 596.
        Hersey writes uncommonly well. Except for Daphne, the
    characterization in the novel is satisfyingly complex, and
    the descriptions of flying are excellent. Hersey seems to
    employ a modified Adlerian psychology.

12 ROLO, CHARLES. "A Hero is a Secret." Atlantic, 204
    (November), 171.
        Hersey could have made a significant point in The War
    Lover, but he has fallen into the American trap of know-how.
    The flight descriptions clutter the book, entrapping the
    better tale waiting to be released. Since Hersey is both
    gifted and conscientious, this is particularly disappointing.

13 STRAIGHT, MICHAEL. "Break-up of a Warrior." New Republic, 141
    (October 12), 17.
        The War Lover employs a structure that evokes tension in
    the reader, stretching the action out through the full novel.
    This tension is of dubious benefit, since we need time to
    reflect on Hersey's powerful but not conclusive argument
    that war is caused by aggressive natures like Marrow's.
    Despite the problems with structure and character revela-
    tion, the novel is a unique recreation of the immediate
    past.

1960 A BOOKS - NONE

1960 B SHORTER WRITINGS

1   BECK, WARREN. "An Ingenious Satire That Hits Its Marks."
    Chicago Sunday Tribune (September 9), p. 3.

1960

The Child Buyer is ingenious, satirizing both teachers
and students through apt dialogue and caricature. The ending of the book is not entirely convincing.

2   BECKOFF, SAMUEL, ed. Four Complete American Novels. New York:
    Globe Book Company, pp. 7-14 and 626-28.
        Includes A Single Pebble as one of four American novels
    by writers whose interest has been primarily in the American
    character; the other selections are The House of the Seven
    Gables, Benito Cereno, and Washington Square. All four
    selections have inherently allegorical or fabular struc-
    tures. Hersey has shown quiet indignation, a kind of Puri-
    tan fervor in the favorable sense of the term, toward
    American values. While he affirms what is true and valu-
    able in our society, he also values the same things in
    other cultures.
        Like several other notable American writers, Hersey was
    trained in journalism. Few have ever moved so quickly as
    he into the realm of serious fiction which comments on con-
    temporary life. His work is "biased" in favor of human
    values; history is placed into a sensitive, humanistic con-
    text. He relies on report as well as analysis, and excels
    as a sympathetic reporter in the tradition of Defoe and
    other journalist-novelists. Hersey has distinctive aware-
    ness and control of language, imaging the Puritan spareness
    he admires. A Single Pebble uses the author's interest in
    cultural anthropology, examining the values and effects of
    technology as he did in The Wall and Hiroshima.

3   DAVIS, ROBERT GORHAM. "An Arrangement in Black and White."
    New Republic, 143 (October 10), 24.
        The Child Buyer is not really a work of the imagination
    because it does not shed light on life or reality. Dia-
    logue is interchangeable among the characters, who turn
    inexplicably into monsters at the end of the book. In many
    ways, the book resembles Advise and Consent; like that
    novel, this work says little about political or social
    events. The "ideas" in the novel are not the concern of
    the reviewer, who must look at the literary qualities of a
    work.

4   FULLER, EDMUND J. Books with Men Behind Them. New York:
    Random House, 240 pp., passim.
        Critics are not the judges of talent, but of what a
    talented writer has achieved. Works have authors behind
    them who must be taken into the evaluation. Hersey's The
    Child Buyer is part of a corrective balancing that is
    needed in our literature, a book which examines modern

1960

problems in a concerned and humane manner as well as in an
experimental form.

5   _____. "Hersey's Dramatic Satire on Education." New York
     Herald Tribune Book Review (September 25), p. 3.
         The Child Buyer is an exceptionally fine novel, done as
     satire somewhat in the Shavian manner. It attacks the edu-
     cational system in this country in order to make its real
     points about the emptiness of cultural values which influ-
     ence the schools. The book falls short of greatness be-
     cause it has an artificial ending.

6   HALSEY, MARGARET. "The Shortest Way with Assenters." New
     Republic, 143 (October 10), 21-22.
         The Child Buyer is the tract at its best, in the tradi-
     tion of Swift's A Modest Proposal. It is the work of a
     writer with principles who is unafraid of emotion and skill-
     ful with words. The work is not really about education;
     with a tone of authority it attacks a whole way of life
     rather than an isolated aspect of it. Hersey ought to run
     for President.

7   HANSEN, CARL F. "Educator vs. Educationist." New Republic,
     143 (October 10), 23.
         Defends American education, stating that The Child Buyer
     achieves satire by sacrificing balance. The book does,
     however, point to a significant problem in contemporary
     life, the fact that knowledge may become so vast and spe-
     cialized that to master it will require the sacrifice of
     normal human experience. This tantalizing question is a
     mark of greatness in Hersey's book.

8   HATCH, ROBERT. "The Brain Market." Nation, 191 (October 8),
     231.
         The Child Buyer demonstrates one of Hersey's skills
     which is also his shortcoming. He is a brilliant technician
     whose works are "polished facsimiles of their forms"; the
     accusation that he senses trends and appraises the market
     is not true. But he is determined to improve his readers,
     and this--combined with his journalistic skills and his
     talent for mimicry--makes him appear to be always manipulat-
     ing the ideas and forms currently in fashion. In satire,
     he may finally have found the device most suited to his
     needs. In reading this work, we experience the devil him-
     self in the form of Jones and feel Hersey questioning our
     honesty too.

1960

9　HUGHES, RILEY. Review of The Child Buyer. Catholic World,
　　192 (December), 181.
　　　　Hersey's satire fails because he offers no clear set of
　　norms to hold in place of those he attacks. It is certain
　　that he opposes the use of education as an instrument in
　　the cold war, and sets up an apocalyptic vision through his
　　imaginary hearings about the sacrifice of the child genius.
　　Yet each potentially normative figure is undercut, leaving
　　in doubt what it is that Hersey is advocating.

10　　＿＿＿. Review of The War Lover. Catholic World, 190
　　(January), 250.
　　　　With intricate, compelling art, Hersey has written a
　　searing indictment of war. It is not a tract, for it ex-
　　hibits narrative excellence and selectivity in persons and
　　events depicted. The book contains an appropriate amount
　　of realistic detail.

11　HUTCHENS, JOHN K. "and What Has Made John Hersey So Angry?"
　　San Francisco Chronicle (October 6), p. 4.
　　　　The Child Buyer is bloodless on the surface, but Hersey's
　　own blood bubbles and rages beneath the words. It is clear
　　that the writer never intended a traditional novel, but
　　rather a satire in the tradition of Voltaire and Orwell.
　　He succeeds in creating a fantastic, yet plausible,
　　nightmare.

12　MACDONALD, DWIGHT. "Masscult and Midcult." Partisan Review,
　　27 (Spring), 203-33.
　　　　Macdonald distinguishes between masscult and midcult.
　　Masscult writing contains a built-in reaction, but has the
　　touch of genius which masses recognize in their own way;
　　examples are Sandburg and Byron. Midcult is formula writing,
　　also containing a built-in reaction, but lacking in stand-
　　ards. Hersey belongs in this group, along with Steinbeck,
　　Marquand, Buck, Irwin Shaw, and Wouk. Midcult is the kind
　　of writing found in magazines such as Saturday Review,
　　Harper's, and The Atlantic Monthly. Midcult is a corruption
　　of High Culture which substitutes faith for cleverness,
　　moralizing for talent. One magazine which avoids the dan-
　　gers of midcult is The New Yorker, where editors work from
　　a formula which reflects their own ideas rather than those
　　imposed by fear of their readers.

13　McDONNELL, T. P. "The Death of the Imagination." Commonweal,
　　73 (December 16), 323.
　　　　In reviewing The Child Buyer, the writer states that even
　　though the novel is deficient in many ways, it has an almost

1960

frightening closeness to real events. The numerous carica-
tures represent various parts of a massive breakdown of intellectual and moral integrity. Mansfield, for example, is
the ineffectual humanist; Skypack, the politician as Philis-
tine; Dr. Gozar, the irreducible rationalist, and Barry, the
exploited product of Scientism. Perkonian is a new type,
the alienated primitive, who needs his own book. In the
long monologues of Barry and Dr. Gozar, we see the controlled and desperate effort to keep alive the human imagination, the child as poet. McDonnell draws a parallel
between Hersey's "forgetting chambers" and the "millions
and millions of pictures" which assault children through
television.

14   NORDELL, ROD. Review of The Child Buyer. Christian Science
      Monitor (September 29), p. 11.
            This is a harsh, satiric work reminiscent of Swift,
      offering uncomfortable absurdity and pressing questions.
      Its closeness to actual truth is also uncomfortable, as
      Hersey drew from his work with the Woodrow Wilson Founda-
      tion for his characterization of the fate of the gifted
      child in our society. Irony sometimes is misunderstood,
      and in this case Hersey's essay "Education in the Nation's
      Service," published by the Woodrow Wilson Foundation, can
      give helpful clues to the novel's meaning.

15   ROWLAND, STANLEY J., JR. Review of The Child Buyer.
      Christian Century, 77 (November 16), 1346-47.
            The Child Buyer is a moral piece with a sense of human
      depravity akin to that in The Deer Park, but it does not
      supply the full expression of the Protestant imagination.
      The Catholic tradition in European literature has no counter-
      part yet in our literature. A book like Hersey's is a deriv-
      ative of the Christian view, informed by the moralism and
      humanity of that view and also possessing a sharp wit. It
      is lively, polished and provocative; Hersey was correct to
      use satire. He avoids the heaviness present in The War
      Lover whenever moral issues overwhelmed characterization.

16   SKINNER, B. F. "May We Have a Positive Contribution?" New
      Republic, 143 (October 10), 22.
            States that The Child Buyer fails to make a positive
      contribution because Hersey's anger does not lead the
      reader to constructive action. The book is based on the
      outmoded myth of the intellectual hero.

17   SMITH, WILLIAM JAY. "The Truly Handicapped." New Republic,
      143 (October 10), 25-26.

Hersey's book tells the truth about our anti-intellectual
society, in which being "gifted" is a "problem" comparable
to other "handicaps." The remedies proposed for educational
problems include subordination of the intelligence to the
demands of a machine age. Hersey has problems satirizing
educationists because they satirize themselves so completely,
but he makes an important point about a major contemporary
problem.

18   STANTON, FRANK. "Parallel Paths." Daedalus, 89, no. 2,
      347-53.
      Discussing the relationship of intellectuals with the
mass media, the writer states that the media need the en-
lightened criticism of the intellectuals, but the latter
need to look at facts before condemning the media. Book-
of-the-Month Club is an institution misjudged by the intellectuals (who actually want to keep the domain of ideas
from mass accessibility). The quality of book selections
is impressive; Hersey is among a number of fine writers
distributed.

1961 A BOOKS - NONE

1961 B SHORTER WRITINGS

1   ANON. Review of The Child Buyer. Times Literary Supplement
     (London) (March 10), 149.
     Hersey will inevitably be compared with Swift, though
his passionate humanitarianism is not much like the education of the Houynhnms. But it is correct to insist that he
has written "a quite brilliant satire, savage, bitter, and
at times very funny."

2   BURTON, ARTHUR. "Existential Conceptions in John Hersey's
     Novel: The Child Buyer." Journal of Existential Psychol-
     ogy, 2 (Fall), 243-58.
     After quoting extensively from The Child Buyer, the
writer declares that the book is fiction with reality
solidly behind it, showing the condition of contemporary
education and the problem of human existence. Hersey is
one of those writers who can state more fully the nature
of human life than the social sciences can. Hersey's book
contains commentary on existential problems which affect
educational philosophy and have ramifications in existential psychiatry and the field of education.
     The book tells an unhappy tale, covering the conceptual
problems of education--teacher's role, learning theories,

1961

ultimate goal--and the educational "world," the social and
existential assumptions behind formal education. Hersey's
characterization of educators, unfortunately taken as ex-
aggeration, shows them to be people who identify with, in-
corporate, and introject the children they teach so that
neither they nor the children have a clear sense of existence. Both the strong and the weak are guilty, those who
persecute Barry and those who try to nurture him. Each
has a price, until the adults' capitulation corrupts even
the child himself. Becoming an adult means surrendering
one's values.

Little has been said about the phenomenological "world"
of education. Hersey shows how education kills creativity,
the self's recognition of its sanity. The educators in the
book have never tapped their own powers, living instead
through the children. Perhaps, outside of the realm of
fiction, this is why teachers are held in low esteem in
the society; they are perceived as non-creative people.
We seem to keep creative people out of the classroom deliberately. Educators blame public conservatism for this, but
as Hersey shows in the novel, they really cling to the se-
curity of a non-creative existence. Education demands "the
idealistic, the humanistic and the incorruptible
personality."

The problem is that learning theory cannot offer a proper
technique for achieving the necessary improvements in education. Incorporated into general learning theory, Gestalt
and purposive behaviorism have lost their strength. Too
much of Pavlov survives. Human beings are complex organ-
isms affected by language, culture, and higher level cogni-
tive processes. Psychologists should emphasize the unity
of man and the world rather than devoting all of their time
to adjustment processes. A teacher who stands for all that
is human in culture can convey this unity. Overuse of ma-
chines in teaching plays to our wish for escape, for Nirvana.
A new humanism in teaching the gifted is especially needed,
yet teachers are not models for this. Until they have
"presence" as humans, the children cannot learn from them,
yet education courses do not help people to grow in this
way. As we lose the children to full humanity, we lose
humanity too.

3   McDONNELL, THOMAS P. "Hersey's Allegorical Novels." The
    Catholic World, 182 (July), 240-45.
        Hersey seems to possess a sense of conscience which is
    unusual among contemporary novelists. Unlike his peers,
    Hersey is not simply recording his own particular experien-
    tial statement, but has a consciousness that he is making a

moral statement. It is, however, this "supraconscience" of sorts which comes dangerously close to reducing his novels to morality tales. Working in this moral sphere, a novelist must run the risk that he may begin to see people as embodied abstractions of his ideas.

Hersey may be said to write "allegories of a modern mind in search of salvation." The form he uses often is documentation. The Wall compares with James Agee's Let Us Now Praise Famous Men because both books have an authentic sense of compassion. Rachel Apt is an over-sentimentalized earth-mother, but the other characterizations in The Wall are memorable. The novel fails only in the sense that the tragedy of the European massacre is too great for the mind to encompass. The only American novel addressing this phase of Western disintegration, The Wall insists on the survival of human values. In The War Lover, Hersey suggests that unsympathetic characters are the ones responsible for war, linking his moral passion to an unsound idea.

In The Child Buyer, Hersey combines his talent for literature in journalistic form with his sense of moral responsibility. The book stands on a forceful idea and also contains a true narrative. Hersey manages to depict the Dionysian and the Appolonian sides of experience. Like other novels of ideas in America, the book puzzles or annoys critics. The Child Buyer really resembles European works which see the human situation in a solid cultural tradition without succumbing to nihilism. As Hersey develops beyond the point of allegory into complexity, he may produce a universal work.

4   WEBB, W. L. Review of The Child Buyer. Guardian (March 10), p. 8.
    Hersey chose a form suited to his purpose, since the documentary tone gives the "cutting edge of actuality," but some of the more bizarre science fiction touches are unfortunate. The work has more imagination behind it than do most tracts, and has been declared recommended reading by the President's Committee on National Aims.

1965 A BOOKS - NONE

1965 B SHORTER WRITINGS

1   ANON. "To Feel What Wretches Feel." Time, 85 (January 29), 94.
    Hersey's best novels, A Bell for Adano, The Wall, and A Single Pebble, are lightly fictionalized stories taken

1965

from contemporary history. His non-journalistic attempts
at creative writing, The Marmot Drive and The Child Buyer,
are clearly failures. With White Lotus, Hersey seems to
have abandoned his hopes to become a serious artist and
settled for Book-of-the-Month Club quality. Because of his
well-recognized name and his use of a contemporary contro-
versy for the material of his historical allegory, he has
succeeded at this mediocre project. An epigram would have
equalled the insight of his novel.

2   HALE, HOPE. "History with a Shade of Difference." Saturday
    Review, 48 (January 23), 43.
        With White Lotus, Hersey has again sought a monumental
    subject comparable in importance to those of Hiroshima and
    The Wall. It is a rich, absorbing tale whose narrator and
    protagonist is appealing and informative. The depiction
    of whites, however, is heavily dependent on stereotypes
    about the Negro race. A more imaginative treatment indi-
    vidualizing the enslaved group would have enhanced the
    parable.

3   JANEWAY, ELIZABETH. "The High Price of Good Intentions."
    Christian Science Monitor (February 4), p. 11.
        In White Lotus, Hersey is telling, not revealing. He is
    convinced, angry, and close-minded about racial discrimina-
    tion. Though he should not be judged by the standards of
    fiction, his work is not equal to that of Swift or Bunyan.
    White Lotus herself is merely a passive amalgam of black
    history, though the creation of the character and even the
    entire book show considerable creativity.

4   KLEIN, MARCUS. "The Perils of White Lotus." The Reporter,
    32 (February 25), 54.
        Hersey translates an impressive amount of political,
    sociological, and psychological fact about our society into
    a Chinese context. But the parable of White Lotus dissolves
    issues into painless truisms which miss some of the subtler
    integration issues. Violence is implicit in the non-violent
    protest techniques used by contemporary civil rights activ-
    ists, but Hersey omits this from his solution. The fact
    that he reads the racial issue as essentially a sexual con-
    frontation reveals more about Hersey than about history.

5   MORGAN, EDWIN. "Sleeping Birds." New Statesman, 69 (June 25),
    1018.
        In White Lotus, Hersey has found a way to deal with the
    problems of the contemporary political novel, producing one
    of the most remarkable books to come out of the current
    vigorous phase of the American novel. The book examines

the nature of freedom, its cost, and the possible methods
of obtaining it as represented by Nose, Peace, Dolphin, and
Rock. The picture of the varied yet stratified Chinese
society is brilliant, and effectively images the deeply
felt theme of the story. The book is Hersey's "most creative and rewarding novel."

6   MURRAY, MICHELE. Review of <u>White Lotus</u>. <u>Commonweal</u>, 81
    (March 5), 743.
        The narrative is straightforward and detailed, revealing
    Hersey's affection for pre-Communist China. Even where his
    concoction is weak, as in other books, he can produce a
    novel which is completely professional. The experience of
    the slaves, however, is made to seem less horrible than it
    probably was, making this story of more interest to whites
    than to blacks.

7   RYAN, F. L. Review of <u>White Lotus</u>. <u>Best Sellers</u>, 24
    (February 1), 414.
        The novel is rich in detail and wide in scope, but it
    somehow does not convey the passion and turbulence implicit
    in the condition of the slave. The Prologue and Epilogue
    alone seem to carry the dual longing and despair which one
    expects, and these employ an interesting rhetoric of silence
    to do so. The massive story between the Prologue and Epi-
    logue does not equal the intensity of these sections, yet
    it too has its value and should not be missed. Hersey in-
    sists that slavery is universal and takes such forms as
    ignorance, racism, and poverty.

8   WEEKS, EDWARD. "The Spirit Enslaved." <u>Atlantic</u>, 215
    (February), 136.
        <u>White Lotus</u> has a powerful beginning, a tedious middle,
    and a moralistic end. The writer states, "I must have peo-
    ple to believe in if I am to suffer so long a text."

<u>1966 A BOOKS - NONE</u>

<u>1966 B SHORTER WRITINGS</u>

1   ALDRICH, NELSON. Review of <u>Too Far to Walk</u>. <u>Book Week</u>
    (March 13), p. 5.
        Compares Hersey's book to Kenneth Keniston's <u>The Uncom-
    mitted</u>. The fictionalized treatment of the new generation
    fails to achieve seriousness. Scientific observers like
    Erikson, Riesman, Arendt, and Goodman do a better job.
    Most of our best novelists have recognized that reality is

1966

made up, in part, of some problems that are insoluble and
some that are ridiculous---and have left the field of social
commentary. Since Hiroshima--the prototype of In Cold
Blood--Hersey has generally written novels of social concern, imbued with a moral sensibility unmistakable in its
liberalism. The Child Buyer, though grounded in careful
research, is weirdly improbable science fiction. He re-
peated this kind of error in Too Far to Walk; with all of
the research to work with, he embodied his statement in the
legend of Faust! The book lacks Faust's aggression, but
has Keniston's alienation. John's soul belongs to Satan
while his wishes go unfulfilled. But a Hersey hero must
triumph. The LSD nightmare is hell--for the reader. Even
Hersey's usual liberal message is fudged. "Hersey...writes
like a tolerant father who is sincerely trying to understand what all the fuss is about, only to conclude that
there really needn't be any fuss after all."

2   ANON. "Pop Faust." Newsweek, 67 (March 14), 104.
        Hersey nearly succeeds in writing a believable and rele-
     vant fantasy. Too Far to Walk has some outstanding sections
     which capture the dilemma of the young, such as the charac-
     terization of Mona and the surfing scene. The Walpurgisnacht,
     however, is a failure, as is the adolescent dialogue at the
     end in which John vanquishes Breed. This last scene is a
     mere parody of the great Faustian endings of the past.

3   BUITENHUIS, PETER. "Sophomore Slump." New York Times Book
        Review (March 13), 4.
        Too Far to Walk is unusual and witty, with an uncanny
     exactness in dialogue which is the more remarkable because
     Hersey wrote the book before becoming Master of Pierson
     College. The sudden switch to fantasy one quarter of the
     way through the story is hard to understand. It does cap-
     ture the mood brilliantly, but it fails to deal with the
     serious issues of the theme.

4   CURTIS, C. MICHAEL. "John Hersey's Sermon Disguised as a
        Novel." Christian Science Monitor (March 17), p. 8.
        Too Far to Walk is a thin novel, but a deeply felt ser-
     mon. Hersey shows existential self-indulgence short of
     merit, endorsing a "disciplined acceptance of life's
     labors."

5   DAVENPORT, GUY. "Deep Waters and Dark." National Review
        (May 3), p. 424.
        States that in Too Far to Walk Hersey has perceived the
     Puritan influence in the protest of the young. Sin is

36

viewed as intolerable in others, though secretly experienced
by the apparently virtuous. The orgy scene in the novel recalls "Young Goodman Brown." Hersey is not alone in observing the strain of Puritan attitudes; Jung, too, observed it.
With his experienced touch as a storyteller, Hersey achieves
what newspapers cannot, showing the exclusivity and deeply
selfish nature of youthful rebellion. It is too bad Hersey
didn't show another contemporary fad, shoplifting, and the
way the young would react to a parent's being involved in
it. This book is unlike other popular novels about current
subjects; it will be a paperback, required reading in human-
ities courses, and probably a film.

6   GROSSMAN, EDWARD. "Son of Faust." New Republic, 154
    (March 26), 21.
        In his most didactic book to date, Hersey writes fiction
    that offers a "slightly worried but ultimately reassuring
    and rational morality." Too Far to Walk takes its subject
    matter almost from the daily paper. Few of the young will
    be interested in Hersey's lesson.

7   HICKS, GRANVILLE. "The Undergraduate Faust." Saturday Review,
    49 (March 19), 29.
        In a review of Too Far to Walk, the writer states that
    Hersey's use of the Faust myth somewhat weakens his portrayal
    of the anomie of the young. His accuracy in describing
    youth, especially in the chapter on LSD, is remarkable. He
    would have done better to trust his own story rather than
    tying it to symbol and legend.

8   REILLY, ROBERT T. Review of Too Far to Walk. America, 114
    (March 12), 358.
        Hersey is at his best when he is a satirist, but this
    novel contains some unfortunate moralizing as well as clever
    satire. Nonetheless, the book is enjoyable reading.

9   SANDERS, DAVID. "John Hersey: War Correspondent into Novel-
    ist," in New Voices in American Studies, edited by Ray B.
    Brawne. Lafayette, Indiana: Purdue University Press,
    pp. 49-58.
        Traces Hersey's development from reporter to fiction
    writer, asserting that his use of topical themes and affirm-
    ative tone make him a writer critics do not appreciate.

10 STERN, DANIEL. "Notes on Reputation." Harper's Bazaar, 232
    (April), 120.
        The very name "John Hersey" brings a multitude of asso-
    ciations, including World War II, Warsaw, Hiroshima. He has

1966

always exhibited a certain conflict between the moralist
and the artist in his make-up, but Too Far to Walk reveals
an unexpected resource of charm and humor. "It is a funny,
concerned book, finally more tract than novel. But the
picture of the obsessions of today's youth sounds and feels
uncannily right."

1967 A BOOKS

1   SANDERS, DAVID. John Hersey. Twayne's United States Authors
    Series, edited by Sylvia Bowman. New York: Twayne Pub-
    lishers, Inc., 159 pp.
        Hersey is really different from other contemporary writ-
    ers, with an approach that does not center on self-definition
    in relation to social forces. In his development as a
    writer, he has moved from correspondence into fiction with-
    out displaying a clear pattern or scheme of development,
    though his career has some parallels to that of Dos Passos.
    Only the theme of survival, urgently expressed, unites his
    varied works. As a writer in the thirties, Hersey would
    have been widely acclaimed.
        Hersey's biography indicates the source of his sympathetic
    and uncomplicated response to contemporary events, but he
    has not simply duplicated in print the evangelical careers
    of his parents. His creative drive has been the need to
    explain human events and the urge to survive in the face of
    annihilation. His three books of the war years, Men on
    Bataan, Into the Valley, and A Bell for Adano, show his
    entertaining skill and his quick and forceful reporting
    techniques, but on the whole they indicate that Hersey had
    to write too much too soon.
        Hiroshima was both a book and an event by which Hersey
    may have influenced history as well as reported it. Sus-
    pense and understatement are means by which Hersey demon-
    strates the individuality of the random survivors and the
    horror of the Bomb. Another book about the war, The Wall,
    is usually regarded as Hersey's best achievement, but it is
    hard to understand how one of Hersey's books can even be
    compared to another. In writing the book, however, Hersey
    grappled in a major way with the creative process, producing
    more than fifty vivid and individualistic characters.
    Levinson, his most ambitious characterization, conveys both
    honest reporting, sympathy, and a strong affirmation of
    life. As opposed to a writer like Leon Uris, Hersey knew
    thoroughly the contemporary historical context in which he
    himself wrote, and his creation, Levinson, likewise knows
    thoroughly the historical traditions from which he writes.

The Wall shows the advantages of Hersey's journalistic training, but moves beyond it into the complexity necessary for serious fiction.

After the war years, Hersey moved into a period of social and political action, working to improve education and to guarantee the artist a more secure place in society. The first book of this period, The Marmot Drive, is an oblique attempt to explain contemporary life. The negative reviews did not damage Hersey, and his next book, A Single Pebble, is one of the best short novels written in this country since the war. It skillfully combines purpose with technique to give a vision of human history through a single, enduring, mysterious memory. Patience, aspiration, grandeur, and pain are the means by which human beings affirm life.

The War Lover is Hersey's analysis of the events he had reported in his early career. It defies the usual interpretation found in the writings of Hemingway and Mailer, stressing the individual's responsibility for what happens to others and to oneself. The complicated exposition gives both suspense and development to the tale told by one of fiction's most unusual heroes, Boman. His sensitive examination of what he is doing causes the hope that Hersey will produce another such protagonist. Drawing on another facet of his experience, Hersey next wrote The Child Buyer, successful despite its flaws in arguing the "unliberal" position that democratic ideals do not necessarily promote excellence in education. Attacks on the book usually reflect ironically on the reviewer's ideas.

The dominant contemporary struggle for survival in peace is imaged in White Lotus. Drawn from survival tales collected in Here to Stay, the book is an abstraction rather than a parable about the Negro experience. The unfashionable book, set in a specific although imagined place, and clearly designed to make a political statement about the prevailing issue of racism, is another refusal by Hersey to enter into critically acceptable forms.

Although Hersey unaccountably has evoked little critical interest, he has received praise from a few notable writers. He actually exemplifies, in his affirmation, commitment, and vitality, a recoil from the contemporary society such as Hassan describes in Radical Innocence.

1967 B SHORTER WRITINGS

1   ANON. "From Esmé with Love and Squalor." Time, 89 (March 17), 110.
     Under the Eye of the Storm is Hersey's best book since A Bell for Adano. His narrative is strong, and his theme

1967

is profound and true. He succeeds in unveiling private
myths of contemporary people, with powerful final irony.

2   CASSILL, R. V. Review of Under the Eye of the Storm. New York
    Times (March 19), p. 4.
        Both the allegory and the realism of this novel are un-
    convincing. The allegory is confused and intermittent in
    the vein of psychological realism; the characterization is
    as stiff and thin as allegory.

3   FIXX, JAMES F. Review of Under the Eye of the Storm.
    Saturday Review, 50 (March 18), 33.
        As he did in The War Lover, in Under the Eye of the
    Storm Hersey tells an exciting yarn which also shapes into
    a moral tale. When he is at his best, his writing has the
    power and verve of life itself. This novel is not as com-
    fortably clear as a medieval morality tale; its philosophical
    underpinnings are complex, and sometimes nearly overwhelm
    the story. But on the whole, it is a haunting work of the
    imagination.

4   HILL, W. B. Review of Under the Eye of the Storm. America,
    116 (May 6), 702.
        Hersey tells a gripping story, yet never resolves the
    conflicts, or even reveals whether they are more than the
    protagonist's imagination.

5   ROBBINS, CORINNE. "Listen to the Wind." Book Week
    (April 23), p. 9.
        Under the Eye of the Storm fails as a novel because it
    has no quest. Hersey's description of the hurricane and
    the small boat caught in it is excellent, but nothing hap-
    pens to his characters because of their experience. The
    novel has no ambiguity.

6   SCHMIDT, SANDRA. "Ripples, Not Waves." Christian Science
    Monitor (April 13), p. 11.
        Under the Eye of the Storm sets up a contrast between
    the compelling power of an ocean storm and the inner turmoil
    of a human being. The insight about the human condition
    which results from the contrast seems rather trifling in
    view of the effort expended. Hersey's main character, Tom
    Medlar, is a complex and intriguing person.

7   SULLIVAN, RICHARD. "Flick and Dottie Afloat." Critic, 25
    (June), 78.
        Suggests a comparison of Under the Eye of the Storm with
    the best of writing about storms; Conrad's Typhoon is an

example, though Hersey is not competition for Conrad. The novel attempts to move on two levels, with a noticeable shift from people to storm at frequent intervals. It is not thoroughly integrated nor always engrossing, but has drama and engaging characterization; the book deserves plain respect as a rewarding piece of fiction.

8   WARNER, JOHN. Review of Under the Eye of the Storm. Harper, 234 (May), 116.
    Hersey is a reporter whose book lacks one shred of plot. His characters are types, not flesh and blood; Tom is out of touch with life, yet lacks the insight to realize it. Hersey's style saves him, since it is clean and sure. His probing journalistic eye and firm control yield an impressive description of the storm despite the cardboard figures which inhabit it.

9   WEEKS, EDWARD. Review of Under the Eye of the Storm. Atlantic Monthly, 219 (April), 141.
    Calls Hersey "a man of intense sympathy and increasing imaginative power" who brings less insularity to his work than many contemporary writers. After his compassionate works of the war years, Hersey needed to find themes from New England, but it took him fifteen years to do so. Under the Eye of the Storm is powerful, admirable writing which creates a bond of believability as the storm wrenches the couples apart and then passes.

1968 A BOOKS - NONE

1968 B SHORTER WRITINGS

1   ANON. Review of The Algiers Motel Incident. Saturday Review, 51 (July 6), 24.
    It is unfair to compare this book with Hersey's great documentary, Hiroshima. The implications of atomic warfare are clearer than those of racial enmity and rioting. The mosaic pattern of narration does not make things any clearer. But he does succeed in pointing out that there is not equal justice in the courts of this nation. The fact that both the victims and the police led circumscribed lives is also an important message.

2   CONOT, ROBERT. Review of The Algiers Motel Incident. New York Times Book Review (July 7), 3.
    Hersey reaches a verdict even though all of the evidence about the murders has not been gathered yet. The structure

1968

of the book is somewhat confusing, with Part 5 providing a
rich context for events. Since Hersey is a major talent
with a strong reputation, he will not suffer for having
published his work before it was ready.

3 HENTOFF, NAT. "Waking Up the White Folks Again." New
   Republic, 159 (November 8), 36-39.
       Hersey's account of injustice toward blacks in The
   Algiers Motel Incident is motivated by his innocent and
   mistaken conviction that telling whites about it will effect
   change. Only the involved complexity of a Norman Mailer can
   create journalism which goes beyond ordinary reportage. The
   books which will truly have an effect will be those written
   by blacks for blacks.

4 MARSH, PAMELA. "Hersey's Hot Summer." Christian Science
   Monitor (July 3), p. 11.
       After investigating the Detroit riots, Hersey decided
   that the hours described in The Algiers Motel Incident were
   a microcosm of the conditions which caused the entire period
   of violence in the city. With superb interviewing skill, he
   drew out both the black citizens and the white police offi-
   cers involved, presenting vivid highlights of the shooting
   and the investigations. His intent is to stir our con-
   sciences with things that need to be said, an approach which
   has its own dangers.

5 MITGANG, HERBERT. Review of The Algiers Motel Incident.
   Saturday Review, 51 (July 6), 24.
       Hersey's method adds to the confusion surrounding the
   incident, and he does not give proper credit to the police
   for arresting and bringing to trial their own colleagues.
   He does succeed in driving home the point that blacks
   do not presently receive justice in the legal system, and
   he reveals aptly one of the causes of racial tension, the
   narrow lives of both black and white victims.

6 SCHLESINGER, STEPHEN. "Shoot-up in Detroit." Atlantic, 222
   (September), 124.
       Hersey took a risk in writing about the Algiers Motel
   incident because the event is an assault on the conventional
   imagination. It reveals the worst sores of society. While
   one must credit Hersey for his moral outrage and determina-
   tion to expose the police, his book lacks a necessary continuity. He should have waited until the trial had been
   held, though it is clear he wanted to affect the outcome of
   it.

7   SCHROTH, RAYMOND A., S.J. Review of The Algiers Motel Inci-
    dent. America, 119 (August 17), 108.
        Hersey has written a "chaotic collage" which he might
    entitle "Racism, U.S.A." Due to his haste, and probably
    to his integrity, the book avoids using factual horror as
    aesthetics. Like the Kerner Report and The Autobiography
    of Malcolm X, the work ought to be required reading for all
    Americans.

8   SOKOLOV, R. A. Review of The Algiers Motel Incident. Newsweek,
    72 (July 1), 88.
        Hersey's skillful use of available evidence builds a
    strong case against the inherent racism of United States
    courts. His best work is a sketch of Auberey Pollard, one
    of the black youths killed in the incident.

9   WEEKS, EDWARD. Review of The Algiers Motel Incident.
    Atlantic, 222 (August), 92.
        Hersey seems to make an issue of white sadism versus
    black innocence, but as this tangled narrative proceeds
    this thesis becomes unclear. The book has the fragmentary
    pattern of the victims' lives, and the reader must thread
    his way among witnesses who lie or are confused or illiter-
    ate. The account of white "justice" is on surer ground,
    for it is clear that the authorities were determined to
    free the police.

1969 A BOOKS - NONE

1969 B SHORTER WRITINGS

1   FIEDLER, LESLIE. "No! in Thunder," in The Novel: Modern
    Essays in Criticism. Edited by Robert Murray Davis.
    Englewood Cliffs, New Jersey: Prentice-Hall, pp. 311-23.
        States that serious fiction must be negative in order to
    meet its essential moral obligation. The Grapes of Wrath
    is the prototype of books which are pious tracts disguised
    as social reports. Writers of the Liberal Protest Novel,
    who believe that social conscience and success are somehow
    not mutually exclusive, include Shaw, Hersey, Schulberg,
    and Michener. These writers express the belief of the
    middle class, which is a sentimental adherence to slightly
    left-of-the-center ideas. Hersey, Shaw, and others become
    "soft-sell defenders of the dark-skinned peoples," actually
    insulting the groups they depict. Writers such as Bellow,
    Malamud, Baldwin, and McCarthy have no room for this pious
    sentimentality. The greatest American work, The Sound and

1969

the Fury, gives form to absurdity, taking the "no" to its
ultimate limits.

2 FRENCH, WARREN. "Fiction: A Handful of Survivors," in his
   The Forties: Fiction, Poetry, Drama. Deland, Florida:
   Everett/Edwards, Inc., pp. 7-32.
       The United States has produced few "war novels" with
   literary merit. Those that are great, including The Red
   Badge of Courage and A Farewell to Arms, depict initiation
   of a sensitive individual into a more profound understanding of reality. The sensitivity demanded in writing literature is generally incompatible with the dispositions required
   to fight in a war. Critics who think of the novel as chronicle or panorama have admired the novels of James Gould
   Cozzens and John Hersey, but such a definition of the novel
   is not acceptable. Hersey is an able reporter, but his
   novels fall in the category of "timely soap opera." Hersey
   descends from a line of preachers; he wants to pound morals
   into us.

3 GOLDMAN, ERIC F. "The President and the Intellectuals," in
   The Tragedy of Lyndon Johnson. New York: Alfred A. Knopf,
   pp. 418-75.
       Describes the White House Festival of the Arts, including
   Hersey's role in it. Instead of withdrawing as did Robert
   Lowell when the bombing of North Viet Nam was undertaken,
   or stating that the occasion was separate from politics,
   as did Saul Bellow, Hersey attended the festival and read
   from Hiroshima. He did this as a political protest; he had
   been invited to read as a novelist. Johnson took as hostil-
   ity Hersey's statements to the press about his ambivalence
   toward attending. He therefore stayed away from the public
   readings, and Hersey could not carry out his intention of
   looking at the President while reading passages of an anti-
   war nature. Mrs. Johnson told Goldman that Hersey should
   read from the novels or not be permitted to take part in
   the occasion, but Goldman refused to censor Hersey or the
   other participants. Though the dialogue between the President and the artists which Goldman had hoped for did not
   take place, the festival was recognized as a gathering together and recognition of the finest living artists from
   every medium.

4 HUDSPETH, ROBERT N. "A Definition of Modern Nihilism: Hersey's
   The War Lover." The University Review, 35 (Summer), 243-49.
       Hersey rejects the point of view expressed often that
   World War II was the struggle between totalitarianism and
   democracy. In A Bell for Adano (1944), The Wall (1950),

and The War Lover (1959) he develops the thesis that the
war was really an effect of modern nihilism. Human urges
to create chaos for its own sake threaten the very existence of human life. These urges result from the attitude
that no values have implicit worth, that values are deter-
mined by the powerful. The dynamism which propels sense-
less frenzies of killing such as that in World War II is
related to political changes. When one leader is replaced
by another, the new one must eradicate old memories and
order. Hannah Arendt and Hermann Rauschning have described
this process, which must deny individuality. The dynamism
ultimately lies outside of politics; values which show
human beings to be above the bestial state must be denied
because they interfere with establishing a system in which
individuals are superfluous.

Like Arendt and Rauschning, Hersey speaks of a world
dominated by nihilistic frenzy. The nihilists fight on
both sides, creating chaos. In The War Lover, Hersey has
progressed from his earlier work to a point where moral
drama is controlled by his aesthetic sense. Boman is an
innocent confronting nihilism in his pilot, but he is not
a wooden symbol.

Marrow, too, is a controlled symbol. He represents the
nihilism which devalues self, others, and the world. He
derives strength from attacking and destroying the beings
he cannot value. Marrow is an attractive figure on the
surface, but Boman learns that his apparent courage is a
huge death wish for all. Humanists represent the only
force which can overcome nihilism. Boman is deficient as
a humanist because he cannot acknowledge Daphne as a separate person; he must acquire moral responsibility toward
her before he can be an effective human being. Daphne's
self-affirmation leads Boman toward his own. Selfless love
must be the basis of value systems. Boman ends the novel
as an initiate who must prove himself as a life lover.
Though nihilism is capable of enormous pressure, individuals can learn their responsibility to love and to act.

5   WIDMER, KINGSLEY. "Notes on the Bomb and the Failure of the
     Imagination," in The Forties: Fiction, Poetry and Drama.
     Edited by Warren French. Deland, Florida: Everett/Edwards,
     Inc., pp. 141-54.
         Examines literary responses to the atomic bomb, suggest-
     ing that these are inadequate to convey the horror of mass
     dehumanization. The bomb itself is an image of a larger
     destruction, the decline of Western culture. A number of
     writers, including Hersey, have tried to use the documentary
     novel to capture the reality of the bomb, but this form is

1969

in itself too polished and edited to image destruction
adequately. In fact, the documentary novel is a reflection
of dehumanizing technology. Hiroshima does not capture
individual response or the moral nature of the issue.

1970 A BOOKS - NONE

1970 B SHORTER WRITINGS

1   BROWN, FRANK C. Review of Letter to the Alumni. Best Sellers,
    30 (November 15), 350.
        Hersey's contribution comes only in the later chapters
    of this book, where he analyzes the problems of the urban
    university in an era of student rebellion and rising costs.
    After his defense of Kingman Brewster and prescription for
    change, one wonders why Hersey is leaving Yale.

2   CURTIS, C. MICHAEL. "Hersey Among the Yalemen." Christian
    Science Monitor (October 22), p. 9.
        Hersey's plea for understanding of the student radical
    is parochial, not profound. He achieves his purpose, argu-
    ing that Kingman Brewster saved Yale from disruption by his
    "principled flexibility." Brewster admitted the injustices
    of the present system, yet refused to yield to absurd
    demands.

3   DeMOTT, BENJAMIN. Review of Letter to the Alumni. New York
    Times Book Review (September 20), p. 7.
        Hersey is not a professional educator nor an "Ivy lifer,"
    but in his five years at Yale he worked hard to reach a
    true understanding of the student experience and its rela-
    tionship to politics. He writes of what is happening with-
    out ambition or strategy, lacking in intellectual penetration
    but excelling in the "extravagance of the heart." His anal-
    ysis is much more helpful than that of other groups and
    individuals.

4   KAMISAR, YALE. "Was Justice Done in the Algiers Motel Inci-
    dent?" New York Times, 4 (March 19), 1.
        After outlining the history of the case, Kamisar men-
    tions that the defense attorney for the accused police
    officers thanked Mr. Hersey for his help with the case.
    Perhaps Hersey proved the officers guilty, but writing is
    not an adversary proceeding. The witnesses for the prose-
    cution did not hold up well in court.

1971 A BOOKS - NONE

1971 B SHORTER WRITINGS

1   KAZIN, ALFRED. Bright Book of Life. Boston, Massachusetts:
     Little, Brown, and Co., 334 pp., passim.
         In a discussion of American novelists and storytellers
     from Hemingway to Mailer, Kazin criticizes recent nonfiction
     novels and documentary forms as a sign of the failure of the
     imagination to deal adequately with mass murder and violence
     in the twentieth century. Indeed, attempts to deal with
     these things may not even be within the realm of art.
     Hersey is one of several journalistic writers alluded to
     throughout the book. Books like his, which deal with real
     events, sometimes dramatize and add to the crises they
     report.

1972 A BOOKS

1   GIRGUS, SAMUEL B. "Against the Grain: The Achievement of
     John Hersey." Ph.D. dissertation, University of New Mexico,
     1972.
         Hersey's books are far more complex in their philosophical
     content and far more individualized in their interpretation
     of life than he has been given credit for by many reviewers
     and by nearly all academic critics. He is in the romantic-
     ironic tradition of Hawthorne as a fiction writer, but his
     political and cultural attitudes have roots in contemporary
     thought. His books display a range of ideas in common with
     such radical critics as Herbert Marcuse, Ivan Illich and
     Charles A. Reich. An important philosophical issue in his
     work is that of the nature of true selfhood, on which his
     comments have affinity with those of Sartre, Tillich, Rollo
     May, R. D. Laing and others. Hersey expresses his view in
     a survival theme which stresses confrontation with the hos-
     tile forces of technological society. True survival comes
     through individual freedom and responsibility. Hersey's
     vision is complex but ultimately affirmative. His complex
     attitude toward art, politics and culture is one reason he
     has not received close critical examination as a serious
     modern writer.
         One reason Hersey has not been an overwhelmingly popular
     writer is that he challenges middle class standards of re-
     spectability well before the changes he advocates occur.
     He also varies forms to suit his vision of the subject,
     rather than working with a formula. He has not been
     accepted by literary critics because of the same independent

1972

patterns of thought. In an age when thinkers emphasize the oppressive nature of social forces, Hersey has continued to portray a world in which individual choice continues to operate when human consciousness is developed.

In A Bell for Adano, Hersey presented a Platonic ideal of America as well as the forces that challenged and changed it. Joppolo teaches the Italians to survive in a consumer society, unwittingly preparing them for the managers who will succeed him. Hiroshima, itself a product of technology, attacks the society which caused the holocaust. The Wall examines the meaning of the ghetto society and the ways in which people transcend fascism. Later books explore various possibilities for love and being. Beginning with The Child Buyer, Hersey has depicted education as one means to full consciousness when it is careful to nurture human potential.

1972 B SHORTER WRITINGS

1 BELL, PEARL K. "Wire-tapping, Nero-style." Christian Science Monitor (March 23), p. 18.
    The Conspiracy is a truncated and unsatisfying examination of power employing the moth-eaten device of letter-writing. Hersey's point seems to be that victims of political events share responsibility for allowing them to occur.

2 WALDRON, RANDALL H. "The Naked, the Dead, and the Machine: A New Look at Norman Mailer's First Novel." PMLA, 87, no. 2 (March), 271-77.
    Mechanization and resistance to it form central thematic principles in modern American literature, especially in novels about World War II. Hersey, like other contemporary novelists, joins the protest against the machine in works such as A Bell for Adano and The War Lover. Drawing on images taken from the world of machines, Hersey and his peers create new forms and metaphors which attempt to demonstrate the human condition threatened by unreason. The Naked and the Dead best exhibits this tension between humanism and technology.

3 WEEKS, EDWARD. Review of The Conspiracy. Atlantic, 229 (March), 106.
    Hersey's examination of power and responsibility is marred by his troublesome method, the use of letters and dispatches for exposition. The book is flawed by its absence of description, yet Latinists will respond to the understatement.

4   YOUNG, ROBERT F., S.J. Review of The Conspiracy. Best Seller,
      32 (April 1), 4.
          Hersey gives a readable and highly accurate account of
      a dark era in history. The book is really a good detective
      story as well.

1973 A BOOKS - NONE

1973 B SHORTER WRITINGS

1   HALTRESHT, MICHAEL. "Dreams, Visions, and Myths in John
      Hersey's White Lotus." Western Georgia College Review, 6
      (May), 24-28.
          The theme of The Wall is that a persecuted minority sur-
      vives if it offers psychological resistance. One of the
      problems in the Warsaw ghetto as Hersey depicts it is that
      the victims of the Nazis are sometimes unconsciously anti-
      Semitic and even collaborate with their oppressors. When
      the Jews' collective ego is weakened, they cannot offer
      effective resistance.
          In White Lotus, Hersey depicts another oppressed, en-
      dangered group. Instead of using the warm, involving diary
      form which created much of the artistry of The Wall, he
      selects another means because his end differs in this work.
      The appeal is intellectual; he is posing a hypothesis about
      why persecuted groups act as they do rather than attempting
      to give the reader a vicarious experience of suffering.
      Hersey is one of a few American writers who apply the in-
      sights of psychoanalysis to the problem of minority oppres-
      sion. The novel is full of dreams, visions, myths, fantasies
      and superstitions which carry the psychoanalytic commentary.
          Examples of the procedure include the dream before the
      "rebellion" in which White Lotus endures self-hatred for
      thinking of stabbing her mistress; the clash of ego and
      counter-ego render her paralyzed. The dream of another
      slave, Grin, depicts the desire to assert individuality
      versus the will of the majority as it has been internalized.
          The collective ego of the oppressed continues to resist
      despite the dangers to the individual. A sense of goal,
      of escape, causes a drive toward health and growth mani-
      fested in dreams, prayers, and fantasies. Peace, for exam-
      ple, has fantasies of freedom and power. The longing for
      spiritual liberty is depicted in images of height, light,
      and fertility. Even a seemingly meaningless song about a
      bride and groom symbolizes the longed-for re-integration
      of the collective personality of the minority.

1973

In contrast to The Wall, Hersey creates a group in White Lotus which keeps its identity, develops goals, and eventually makes a contribution to the larger society. The mystic illumination of White Lotus at the end of the story symbolizes the triumph of those who never accept confinement.

1974 A BOOKS - NONE

1974 B SHORTER WRITINGS

1 HEATH, SUSAN. Review of My Petition for More Space. Saturday Review/World, 1 (September 21), p. 26.
Hersey's novel combines elements of Orwell and of Beckett to present the horrors of overpopulation. Tension, pessimism, and an obstinate hope are part of the story of the waitline, a story which is frighteningly close to being true.

2 HICKS, GRANVILLE. Review of My Petition for More Space. New York Times Book Review (September 22), p. 2.
Hersey is a talented allegorist who succeeds in summing up and dramatizing the horrors of overpopulation through the story of a few hours on a waitline of the future. The climax is an image of bureaucratic tyranny. The book is readable and teaches an important lesson well.

3 LINDSAY, LEON. Review of My Petition for More Space. Christian Science Monitor (October 30), p. 10.
Despite the pessimistic premise on which the plot is based, this book invites the reader to think. Ultimately, it is a positive description of human nature.

4 SLOAN, JAMES PARK. "Hersey's Heroic, Painful Response to the Power of Scarcity." Chicago Tribune Book World (September 15), Section 7, p. 3.
My Petition for More Space is the story of the defeat of the decent but inadequate liberal humanism of Major Joppolo in A Bell for Adano, and of Hersey himself. He is prevented from a strongly condemning statement about modern unreason because of his belief that even his own values are not absolutes. Instead, he has produced a cry of pain in this book, which has space as its central metaphor and also as the central term of a paradox.

1975 A BOOKS

1   HUSE, NANCY LYMAN. "John Hersey: The Writer and his Times."
    Ph.D. dissertation, University of Chicago, 1975.
        John Hersey has been a difficult writer to describe and
    to evaluate. His essentially moralistic and didactic works
    reflect a consistent philosophy of life and art and offer
    complex affirmations of the human condition which the domi-
    nant form of contemporary academic criticism is not well
    suited to judge. This study analyzes Hersey's rhetoric and
    moral imagination in the context of his active role as a
    reporter and social critic. A discussion of unpublished
    essays and letters is included.
        Hersey assumes that his readers are in need of vision,
    which he undertakes to give through the passion of his own
    commitments and his documentary inventiveness. When meas-
    ured by criteria which acknowledge the relationship of a
    writer's life and beliefs to aesthetic forms, Hersey's
    accomplishment can be better understood and appreciated
    than when he is appraised by textual criteria alone. While
    he has self-defined limits, choosing to depict humanity as
    Sisyphus turning to take up his burden by choice, Hersey's
    long and prolific career is interesting in both literary and
    historical terms.
        A close friend of issue-oriented writers such as Lillian
    Hellman and Robert Penn Warren, Hersey has been outspoken in
    his criticism of politics, education, and morals in post-
    World War II America. While Hiroshima (1946) and The Wall
    (1950) established his reputation for liberal humanism and
    reportorial writing, Hersey's subsequent actions and books
    have elaborated on his philosophy that true survival is
    possible and desirable only with the attainment of individ-
    ual freedom within a community which nurtures the creative
    intelligence. The unifying theme of his work, and the one
    which reflects his choice of personal actions and modes of
    storytelling, is the need for and possibility of authentic
    communication. In his novels, the protagonist is a gifted
    communicator, often a writer or storyteller, who interprets,
    dignifies, and actually creates reality through linguistic
    choices. Hersey's nonfiction carries out the moral impera-
    tive of the fiction, combining exhortation with dramatic
    techniques.
        Chronologically considered, Hersey's work reveals his
    growth from an early habit of echoing the editorial position
    of Time and Life to the possession of a vision uniquely his.
    The first four books, Men on Bataan (1942), Into the Valley
    (1942), A Bell for Adano (1944) and Hiroshima (1946) illus-
    trate both Hersey's evolution into a cultural critic and

51

1975

his identification of his major literary theme, the inter-
change of ideas in an open society and the potential of the
artist as agent for change which embodies humanistic truths.
Stories written between the publication of Hiroshima and
The Wall (1950) demonstrate Hersey's increasing preoccupa-
tion with the power and utility of the written word. In
The Wall, still Hersey's most resonant work of fiction, the
writer Levinson is the marrow of the community, receiving
life from the past and present and generating it for the
future. The creation of this character, praised by such
critics as Alfred Kazin, Maxwell Geismar, and David Daiches,
represents Hersey's commitment to the use of serious fiction as a means of rhetorical efficacy with his audience.
   In two successive novels, Hersey creates parables of
annihilation. In the poorly integrated symbolic novel The
Marmot Drive (1953) he examines the effect on the sensitive
individual of an inauthentic culture which places limits on
freedom and truth. The novel possibly reflects the anguish
of the McCarthy period. A Single Pebble (1956) is a successful didactic work which cautions against the devaluing of
the self and the failure to treasure the past. In this
work, Hersey shows himself a master at infusing life into
beliefs which are threatened but not, in his perception,
absent from contemporary life.
   In The War Lover (1959) Hersey presents humanism as the
alternative to destruction, a humanism which depends on the
kind of cultural cross-fertilization which Levinson advo-
cates in The Wall and which Hersey's journalism insists
upon. The Child Buyer (1960), a startling satire of American life and education, suggests that even professed humanists like Dr. Gozar and Barry Rudd must have the sustaining
love of others in order to survive as human beings. The
way to achieve sustaining community is demonstrated by the
rhetoric of Here to Stay (1963), which Hersey used in a
public reading at the White House Festival of the Arts, and
of White Lotus (1967). The heroine of the latter book
attains both individuality and freedom, experiencing a community of support with those she meets of her own enslaved
race and the master race as well. Hersey, as in several
other works, sacrifices suspense in order to move the reader
toward social action, a characteristic Stott says is found
often in documentary forms.
   Too Far to Walk (1966) begins the examination of being
and seeming which seems to allow the individual to believe
in the dignity of human life and society without sacrificing
intellectual credibility. The use of the Faust legend gives
a stability to the possibility of evil without endorsing ex-
tremes of heaven and hell. The conscious willing of

affirmation found in this novel and in <u>Under the Eye of the Storm</u> is supplemented by the nonfiction of this period, <u>The Algiers Motel Incident</u> (1968) and <u>Letter to the Alumni</u> (1970), in which the writer assumes his own moral authority and righteousness and demonstrates it with acts of judgment and prophecy, deliberately intervening in the issues of his time.

Two additional fictions, <u>The Conspiracy</u> (1972) and <u>My Petition for More Space</u> (1974) expand on the notion of the writer's potential, actually arguing that it is central to the well-being of a society. These works imply that the dead communities who reject art cannot be without blame for their self-destruction. But the writers themselves are almost constrained to continue in their truth-telling. The writer who declares himself an outsider cannot fully benefit the world; it is necessary for him to accept some of the responsibility for the kind of life he sees. Hersey's activities on behalf of the Authors' Guild, his participation in The Committee to End Government Secrecy, and other public actions he has taken attest to his sense of moral obligation as an artist. At the same time, he has declined to publicize his work through television shows and extensive interviews.

Hersey has been part of an ancient and needed reportorial tradition, and has carved out a special place somewhere between journalism and popular formulaic fiction. It is not out of order to group him with Steinbeck, Wells, Hellman, and other socially conscious imaginative artists.

1975 B SHORTER WRITINGS

1 KEATES, JONATHAN. Review of <u>My Petition for More Space</u>. <u>New Statesman</u>, 89 (May 16), 668.

Hersey's novel continues the American apocalyptic tradition. Space is imaged thoughtfully, even horrifyingly, though the story cannot really support its own length.

2 WILLS, GARY. Review of <u>The President</u>. <u>New York Review of Books</u>, 22 (October 16), 18.

Hersey uses somewhat highflown metaphors to describe Ford and the Oval Office. He does not choose to reveal that he himself played for Yale while Ford coached there, probably because it would spoil the effect of the "transfiguration scene" at the White House.

1977 A BOOKS - NONE

1977

1977 B SHORTER WRITINGS

1   GARDNER, PETER. Review of The Walnut Door. Saturday Review,
         9 (September 17), 38-39.
            Hersey is at his best in this work of erotic discovery,
         which is both tender and subtle. The story contains an
         optimistic message for contemporaries.

2   LYONS, GENE. "What Remains Is Sexual Melodrama." New York
         Times Book Review (September 18), p. 9.
            In the past, Hersey has tried to examine the effect of
         cataclysmic events, reaching for an audience wider than the
         academic and literary one most serious writers want. The
         Walnut Door seems to depart from his allegorical style,
         telling a fast-paced but somewhat trivial story of two young
         people whose mutual attraction remains a mystery.

3   MARTIN, SYLVIA. "John Hersey's Literary Porn." Chicago
         Tribune (September 11), p. 8.
            Hersey's allegorical novels are often problematic, and
         The Walnut Door is not his best. It is littered with every-
         day obscenities and symbolism, but also displays flashes of
         brilliance and an exciting rhythm. This book is the
         author's experiment with two of the facets of the word
         "craft" which he uses to describe the writing process,
         namely art and trickery. His technical expertise is
         marred by the dishonest ending.

JAMES AGEE
(1909-1955)

Introduction

Agee was born in Knoxville, Tennessee, the son of Hugh James Agee and Laura Whitman Tyler. After his father's death in 1916, Agee was educated at private schools, including Phillips Exeter and Harvard. For much of his adult life, he worked as a journalist, film critic, and film writer, though he had identified his life work as that of a creative writer. During his lifetime, he published only three books: an early volume of poetry, Permit Me Voyage (1934); a nonfiction, Let Us Now Praise Famous Men (1941); and a novella, The Morning Watch (1951). After his death an unfinished work, A Death in the Family (1957), was edited and published by friends. Subsequently, collections of his poetry, short prose, letters and film work have appeared.

Agee's biography is important for both its effect on his work and its effect on his critical reputation. Most of his work is read as an exploration of his past, with the secular strength of his father and the religious ardor of his mother juxtaposed in their marriage, and ultimately merged in Agee himself.

His attractive, complex personality and wide circle of literary acquaintances have resulted in a number of early, personalized comments on his work and lifestyle, such as the devoted editing done by Robert Fitzgerald and David McDowell, and the numerous arguments for or against his work for Time, Life, and Nation. His Harvard friends, fellow Southerners, and close friend Father Flye contributed early, sympathetic commentary on his life and work. Though much Agee criticism is at least partly biographical in nature, the definitive biography being prepared by David McDowell has not yet appeared.

Agee criticism is of three major types. The first considers Agee a failure, for a variety of reasons. The second concedes him a measure of seriousness and even greatness, but ultimately concludes that his ambivalence was essentially self-destructive. The third type, the majority view, finds Agee a rich subject for literary analysis and generally finds consistency, magnanimity, and union of form and content in his work. Since the first dissertation (Jack Behar, Ohio State) appeared in 1963, Agee has increasingly been the subject of academic criticism in the fields of literature, popular culture, and film. A total of twenty books and dissertations have appeared to date.

Interestingly, all three critical estimates of Agee's work appear in the early reviews of his poetry and first full-length nonfiction work, Let Us Now Praise Famous Men, and persist through the seventies. A major factor in Agee criticism has been his relatively early death and the posthumous publication of so much of his work. For that reason, Victor Kramer, who first examined the unpublished papers at the University of Texas, has been the most prolific and possibly the most influential Agee critic outside of the writer's own circle of friends.

Agee's first book, Permit Me Voyage, a collection of poems, drew mixed reviews during its own decade, but his poetry was later cited by both Elizabeth Drew and Joseph Warren Beach for its textual and thematic richness. Let Us Now Praise Famous Men evoked a range of reactions, with most reviewers stating that Agee had attempted the impossible in trying to recreate his state of mind in Alabama. Among those who admired Agee but viewed his life as a failure was Dwight Macdonald, who stated that contemporary American culture made a masterpiece such as Moby Dick no longer possible. Those who admired Agee's first book when it appeared praised him as a poet rather than a writer of fiction or nonfiction.

During the fifties, which saw both Agee's death and the publications of A Morning Watch and A Death in the Family, Agee drew brief commentaries from noted critics such as John Simon, Alfred Kazin, Leslie Fiedler and Richard Chase, in addition to reviews and a few academic articles. Of the critics named, film reviewer Simon was the most enthusiastic and Chase the least. Fiedler identified Agee's talent as essentially "visual," a theme to be explicated in later academic criticism. During this decade, however, Agee's life and work were seen as essentially incomplete, with W. Frohock expressing the view that Agee was one artist, among others, whom the United States has lost to popular media.

The sixties, which marked the start of the strong interest in Agee as a subject for graduate study, began the attempts to reconcile Agee's personality, varied writings, and aesthetic. The tendency to find consistency among these elements can be seen in the work of Jack Behar, Peter Ohlin, Victor Kramer, Samuel Hynes, and others, with the "type two" position that Agee was potentially great but ultimately self-destructive the position of fewer critics, including Alfred Barson and Jeanne Concannon. Articles in support of Agee as a resonant writer became numerous, examining the themes and structure of individual works. The "failure" position was taken by Durant DaPonte, who saw Agee's work as unfruitful quests for identity.

The availability of the unpublished manuscripts at Texas has affected Agee criticism of the current decade, with considerable discussion offered about the integrity of A Death in the Family. Kramer views Let Us Now Praise Famous Men as Agee's major accomplishment and, though critical of some editorial decisions, generally agrees with the editors of the posthumous novel. He has not included the film work in his consideration of the poetry and prose, while Barson and Ohlin have done so. In his 1975 Twayne series volume, Kramer reiterates his earlier thesis that Agee's intention to depict "a personal apprehension of minute intersections of time and place" required the incompleteness for which he has been faulted, while Barson's 1975 revision of his earlier work holds that Agee's best work, parts of Let Us Now Praise Famous Men and A Death in the Family, results from an artistic tension absent from the film work. Separate studies of the film work, however, have related it to Agee's aesthetic as seen in his poetry and prose. A dissenting voice is that of Eliot Silberberg, who states that Agee failed to depict life in art as he had intended. The most recent book-length study, a literary biography by a French scholar, Genevieve Moreau, sees Agee's work as a "dialectic of reconciliation" which arose from his conflicting experiences and beliefs. Moreau states that Agee moved from anger to love, thus joining those who, with Peter Ohlin, view Agee's total career in positive terms.

The wealth of formal analysis Agee has generated, as well as his interest in moral questions, suggests that he meets various sets of criteria used to appraise American authors. Numerous commentators have pointed to the need for a definitive biography, for production of his unused film scripts, and for a continued editing of his unpublished papers, indicating that interest in his contributions is still growing. Wayne Booth's rhetorical criticism and William Stott's analysis of the documentary seem to have affected critical attitudes toward Agee's less conventional forms, generally broadening the base of writings acknowledged as important.

The bibliography includes, I hope, all books and nearly all articles published about Agee. It does not include all reviews, since the wealth of other material required some selectivity. For major studies such as the ones by Kramer, Ohlin and Barson, I have written lengthy annotations in order to present a strong picture of the kind of explication Agee's work evokes and even requires.

For help in preparing this list, I am indebted to Dr. Gertrud Champe for her translation of the Stringher essay.

Writings about James Agee (1940-1977)

1940 A BOOKS - NONE

1940 B SHORTER WRITINGS

1   DREW, ELIZABETH, in collaboration with John L. Sweeney.
     "'Sunday, Outskirts of Knoxville, Tennessee,'" in <u>Directions
     in Modern Poetry</u>. New York: W. W. Norton and Co.,
     pp. 243-49.
          "Sunday, Outskirts of Knoxville, Tennessee" is an example
     of modern craftsmanship in poetry. Sound and image patterns
     are intricately woven throughout the verse. A visual pat-
     tern takes the reader from the pastoral scene to old age
     and death, while a sound pattern moves from soft to harsh
     syllables. The final sounds and the final visual image
     re-echo the original, but in a way suited to the structure
     of the poem. Agee's poem is a "superlative example" of
     representation by suggestion. The balance of the two
     visions is the source of pity.

1941 A BOOKS - NONE

1941 B SHORTER WRITINGS

1   ANON. Review of <u>Let Us Now Praise Famous Men</u>. <u>Time</u>, 38
     (October 13), 104.
          This work is a distinguished failure. Not only is it
     impossible for any author to convey all he feels, but Agee
     prevents the text from succeeding by his bad manners and
     tendency to show off linguistically. When not trapped by
     his self-consciousness, Agee is a poet.

2   BARKER, GEORGE. Review of <u>Let Us Now Praise Famous Men</u>.
     <u>Nation</u>, 153 (September 27), 282.
          The virtues of <u>Let Us Now Praise Famous Men</u> are also its
     vices. In his eagerness to record the present moment, in
     his too generous hospitality toward all things, Agee has
     created a confused clutter of objects instead of a

61

1941

dignified memorial to the three families. At times, however, the individual figures of family members do appear
clearly and accusingly in the text.

3   CORT, J. C.   Review of Let Us Now Praise Famous Men.
    Commonweal, 34 (September 12), 499.
        From time to time, Let Us Now Praise Famous Men presents
    a reasonably good picture of the wretched lives of the
    tenant farmers, both through Agee's sensitive observations
    and Evans' camera recordings. But the work is irreparably
    marred by the repetition, irrelevant detail, and introspec-
    tion which Agee insists on bringing to it. His introspec-
    tion concentrates not only on the ostensible subject of the
    book, but also on virtually everything he may have
    experienced.

4   ETZKORN, L. R.   Review of Let Us Now Praise Famous Men.
    Library Journal, 66 (August), 667.
        The story of the tenant farmers needs to be told. But
    Let Us Now Praise Famous Men includes a mass of unrelated
    and nonsensical material. Some of the extraneous material
    is lunacy, while some of it is beautiful lyric prose--both
    extremes unrelated to tenant life. In addition, some of
    the passages are morally objectionable.

5   RODMAN, SELDEN.   Review of Let Us Now Praise Famous Men.
    Saturday Review, 24 (August 23), 6.
        The writer states that Let Us Now Praise Famous Men is
    realism for those who are not afraid to face the naked
    truth and for those who admit that they do not fully under-
    stand the categories we call "art" and "poetry." Even
    readers with high sensitivity to language and ideas will
    experience a certain degree of rage in the reading of this
    book, wanting to call Agee "an Ezra Pound in Wolfe's cloth-
    ing" or other names which refer to the obliqueness and
    originality of the book. As a book about the relationship
    of art and life, part of its greatness lies in the struc-
    tural failure which contrasts effectively with its moments
    of poetic genius. Unless the country abandons thoughtful
    analysis and poetic insight for extremes such as fascism
    and do-goodism, the book will continue to be read in the
    future (and continue to be disliked).

1945 A BOOKS - NONE

1945 B SHORTER WRITINGS

1   FLYE, JAMES HAROLD. "Reminiscences and Reflections." <u>Holy Cross Magazine</u>, 56 (October), 297-301.

Begins a description of the education available at Saint Andrew's by using Agee's view of education as an ideal and stating that Agee, one of the best writers in America, is the foe of cruelty, hypocrisy, snobbery and any other evil sometimes condoned under the label "education." His sympathy, understanding, and ability to recreate the bonds among human beings make his statement about education, quoted in the article, especially important. In a letter to Father Flye, Agee states that education is really the cause of misunderstanding, and it is guilty of a kind of murder of the individual. This is especially sad, since both science and Christianity, used in conjunction, can free the individual as a human being.

As a teacher at Saint Andrew's, the writer has learned it is important not to carry obedience and conformity too far, noting that Agee as a child was too much an individual to have been able to adjust to an overly rigid system. Christian values and a knowledge of psychology, combined with the general good will of the students at the school, have made Saint Andrew's a place where a reasonably good intellectual and social climate has been maintained. It is especially important not to talk down to children, and to elicit their ideas and views about how they are governed. One difficulty in American education is caused by the desire to educate everyone. Some people cannot achieve in an academic setting, and their efforts to do so, as well as efforts to teach them, range from tragedy to farce.

Over the years, Saint Andrew's produced a number of distinguished graduates. Some of the boys who could not perform well found appropriate work in non-academic fields. Some who were personally difficult matured after they left the school. The general atmosphere at Saint Andrew's was notably friendly, with little emphasis on political matters. This has worked to the school's advantage; it is the business of young people to play rather than to become imbued with an ideology.

1951 A BOOKS - NONE

1951 B SHORTER WRITINGS

1   CHASE, RICHARD. "Sense and Sensibility." <u>Kenyon Review</u> (Autumn), pp. 688-91.

1951

> States that <u>The Morning Watch</u> is an ambitious tour de
> force comparable to Melville's <u>Pierre</u>. It is metaphor and
> myth which is demanding and impossible. Too much metaphor
> for the meaning the work carries gives it "a heavy inert-
> ness." Part of the difficulty is that Agee's language acts
> as "a kind of free-lance, predatory agent," constantly qual-
> ifying and amplifying. Unguarded sensitivity is not enough,
> even with the force of Agee's rhetoric, to create good
> fiction.

1953 A BOOKS - NONE

1953 B SHORTER WRITINGS

1   LEVIN, MEYER. "American Literature through the Picture Tube."
    <u>Reporter</u>, 8 (April 14), 31-33.
        The Ford Foundation "Omnibus" television series on
    Abraham Lincoln, written by James Agee, was the "most orig-
    inal and important work so far created for video." Agee
    depicted Lincoln as a natural saint, showing intimate psy-
    chological details and involving the viewer in the film.
    The series had some self-consciousness, but on the whole
    was a successful experiment, both technically through the
    use of camera for revelation and analysis and artistically
    through symbolic suggestion. It introduced elaborate cos-
    tuming into the documentary.

1957 A BOOKS - NONE

1957 B SHORTER WRITINGS

1   FIEDLER, LESLIE. "Encounter with Death." <u>New Republic</u>, 137
    (December 9), 25-26.
        <u>A Death in the Family</u> is not a complete novel, but has
    been edited to look like one. It alternates between a con-
    trolled novella and a loose saga. Of the two, it is the
    novella which is more like a finished work. Two themes,
    death and the religious conflict, are resolved--but other
    themes such as alcoholism and the family differences remain
    to be dealt with in the saga. Agee's talent is visual
    rather than dramatic. He offers language that stays--
    poetry--and nostalgia without sentiment.

2   FROHOCK, W. M. "James Agee: The Question of Unkept Promise."
    <u>Southwest Review</u>, 42 (Summer), 221-29.

Agee represents a problem current in American letters: the loss of major novelists to commercial media. Both self-searching and crafting were important to Agee; his three books are autobiographical attempts to resolve conflicts between his past in the South and his acquired Eastern identity, while his journalism and film work allowed craft with less self-involvement. His adherence to autobiographical fiction may suggest a limited imaginative range. It is significant that he called himself a "writer" rather than a novelist or artist.

3   KAZIN, ALFRED. "Good-bye to James Agee," in his Contemporaries. Boston: Atlantic Monthly Press, Little, Brown and Co., pp. 185-86, 187.
    Agee gave all of himself to his projects, finding creative opportunities in everything. Journalism and other popular forms may have been his best, since their structures allowed his tenderness and sense of comedy to enter in. He had a tendency when on his own to overwhelm with words, as in Let Us Now Praise Famous Men, which is not a fully realized artistic work and which may be over-rated. His other two fiction books are almost too disciplined, though A Death in the Family is original and individualistic. The father is probably the best characterization in that work, because he is outside of the grief situation.

4   MACDONALD, DWIGHT. "Death of a Poet." The New Yorker, 33 (November 16), 204-21.
    A Death in the Family celebrates the mystery of death illumined by love. Agee is a serious writer, as natural as Mark Twain and full of sensibility rather than intellection. Macdonald calls him "the most broadly gifted writer of my generation," stating that Agee should have done major work but did not. His moral and humorous viewpoint includes a positive attitude toward marriage, and his lack of a pruning editor--such as Perkins in the case of Wolfe--prevented that view from proper shaping.
    One of Agee's significant problems was that his versatile appreciation of literature, cinema and music was incompatible with his times. He led a wasteful, self-destructive life, unable to find the kind of controlling tradition used by writers like D. H. Lawrence. His work for film was distressingly conventional because his real commitment was to literature.
    Like Moby Dick, Let Us Now Praise Famous Men is hard to classify. A Death in the Family is more controlled, but not as great as about half of the earlier work. The control suggests that he was settling and might have fully developed his great gifts. Reprinted: 1962.B8 and 1974.A2.

1957

5   MADDOCKS, MELVIN. "Agee's Last Work." Christian Science
       Monitor (November 14), p. 11.
          A Death in the Family contains the difficult achievement
       of the child's point of view rendered unsentimentally. Less
       a novel than "a pastiche of mood pieces, written in a kind
       of half-scanned prose," the book centers on the child,
       rather than on the father's death. The acquiring of a new
       cap, on the child's scale of values, is a more significant
       event than the accident. Though the book is clearly un-
       finished, lacking transitions and sometimes rhetorically
       static, it has a rare "urge toward the celebrative." Homely
       places and people are depicted affectionately, and the
       Joycean reveries explore the sense of identity in childhood
       roots.

6   RUHE, EDWARD. Review of A Death in the Family. Epoch, 7,
       no. 3 (Fall), 247-51.
          During his lifetime, Agee achieved a notable reputation
       in literature. His first book, Permit Me Voyage, proved
       his confidence and independence. Let Us Now Praise Famous
       Men was both a personal testament and an effective attack
       on those factors in American culture which Agee perceived
       as limiting human achievement. The warmth and anger of the
       book has been somewhat lost on the public, both because of
       its timing--after the thirties--and because of its complex
       structure. The structure may be a rebellion against the
       establishment in literature, just as the content rebels
       against traditional authorities in government, family life,
       and education. Agee's masterpiece remains outside the
       mainstream of American letters, and one may argue that its
       meaning as a work of art and of politics requires that it
       continue to be regarded in this way.
          Agee's last few years were spent in preparing A Death in
       the Family, a book from which his early fury is missing,
       but which contains his continued sense of the dignity and
       power of human life and love. The work is comprised of
       fragments which vary in point of view, intensity, and
       quality. Possibly Agee had not defined his central inten-
       tion. Despite this, the book is one of great distinction
       and reflects Agee's theory of art and generous soul. His
       Blakean doctrine required that he try to convey the wonder
       of life as an immediacy. Sections which best fulfill his
       creed are the great-grandmother scene and the opening scene
       in which father and son return from a Chaplin film.
          Agee's realism is not one of surface appearances. It
       includes a natural sense of metaphor, yielding a trans-
       figured picture of life and a sense of timelessness. The
       tone of the writing is reverent, modest, and above all

accurate. Reality is so convincingly portrayed that questions of style are irrelevant.
    The characters of the novel live in an ordinary mode;
the plot does not force their actions into patterns that
are required by the novelist's intent. Six important chapters omit Rufus, the main character, and describe the events
of the night of the death in a quiet, unobtrusively sym-
metric manner. The section about Jay and Rufus after the
Chaplin show is a cameo of Agee's technique and peculiar
vision. In a kind of Victorian stereotype, Agee uses Mary
as an image of the feminine-genteel impulse and Jay as an
image of freedom touched by loneliness and responsibility.
The qualities Jay exemplifies were the chief aim and subject of Agee's work; he was not really a rebel but a spokes-
man for the affirmation of human reality.

7   SCOTT, WINFIELD TOWNLEY. "Agee's Mature and Masterful Last
      Novel." New York Herald Tribune Book Review (November 17),
      p. 3.
          A Death in the Family fulfills Agee's talent. Let Us
      Now Praise Famous Men will survive, especially if it is
      cut and edited; The Morning Watch foreshadows the last book.
      In fact, much of Agee's early work is obsessed with his
      father's death, the central event of A Death in the Family.
      The irrevocable altering of a world that had seemed real
      and permanent is an experience most human beings have.
      Agee renders it in a lyrical tone saved from sentimentality
      by its factualness. The work builds toward the final mo-
      ment, when the children confront their father in his coffin
      and try to comprehend death. Though unfinished, and some-
      what jarringly edited, the work will be remembered by all
      readers.

1958 A BOOKS - NONE

1958 B SHORTER WRITINGS

1   HAYES, RICHARD. "James Agee: Rhetoric of Splendor."
      Commonweal, 68 (September 12), 591-92.
          Rejecting the separation of feeling from intellection,
      Agee attempted to create a modern consciousness in a pas-
      sionate unity. He had a moral as well as an aesthetic mis-
      sion. In The Morning Watch and A Death in the Family, he
      achieved a "rhetoric of splendor," the honorable in the
      human experience woven into artifact and ever capable of
      being reborn in the reader. His choice of death as a sub-
      ject may indicate that he could not deal with ambivalence,

1958

but his heroic impulses were rendered tragic by his aware-
ness of limitation and loss. He was, ultimately, a poet.
A word for him would be "gentle," as one would call
Shakespeare "sweet."

2 THOMPSON, LOVELL. "Reply to Dwight Macdonald." The New
   Yorker, 32 (February 15), 108.
        In a letter responding to a statement of Dwight Macdonald
   that Houghton Mifflin remaindered Let Us Now Praise Famous
   Men soon after its release, Thompson explains his company's
   policy toward the book. It was kept on lists and demand for
   it recorded until 1953. Houghton published A Morning Watch,
   indicating the company's continued bond with Agee.

1959 A BOOKS - NONE

1959 B SHORTER WRITINGS

1 DAVIS, LOUISE. "He Tortured the Thing He Loved." The Nash-
   ville Tennessean Magazine (February 15), pp. 14-15, 21.
        Agee was a successful writer who never lost touch with
   his Tennessee roots, using his hill country background as
   material for his fiction. He differed from Thomas Wolfe in
   his emphasis on intellect rather than on intuition. His
   film criticism was direct and vivid. Mia Agee, his wife,
   states that his death was the "last thing on our minds."

2 MACDONALD, DWIGHT. "A Way of Death," in his Memoirs of A
   Revolutionist. New York: Meridian Books, Inc.,
   pp. 262-66.
        The reason Let Us Now Praise Famous Men lacks critical
   acclaim while a work like Under the Volcano gets too much
   is that Agee broke highbrow conventions. The defects of
   the work are integral to the strengths. It is comparable
   to Moby Dick is many ways, but the tenants are passive.
   America failed to supply creative force as it did for
   Melville; also, Agee was too involved with the material.
   It does picture the times, however, for we can say with the
   tenants, "How was it we were caught?" We have been trapped
   in joyless work and hurried to war. At least Agee avoids
   the progressive trap. Reprinted: 1962.B8, 1974.A2.

3 SIMON, JOHN. "Let Us Now Praise James Agee." Midcentury, 15,
   no. 6 (November), 17-22.
        Movie critics generally fall into one of two categories:
   the "soft" type who likes half of what he sees, and the
   "hard" type who becomes a primadonna. Even the best of

critics sometimes fall into the trap of looking for reality in what might be art. Agee stood out as a reviewer because he knew film and wrote well, but his chief distinction is that he was "beautifully and tragically humane." Agee on Film demonstrates on every page the conflict of judgment with humanity, the response of both a connoisseur and a struggling human being.

Agee's views on art were part of his views on life, and vice versa. Thus his criticism is written in his own voice, that of a man talking with others. Another virtue of his work is his ability to prophesy and to guide toward the good, such as his comments about television and Neo-realism. He was able to identify and memorialize the outstanding supporting performance or the film which might otherwise have been undeservedly forgotten. He also had the gift of liking the "partly likeable," of seeing relative good even in "trash."

Though one might characterize Agee's film criticism as full of good humor, wit, and poetic perception, it is more accurate to speak of it as a book of love and hate. Agee hated the routine, false and stupid in both life and art, and loved the individual and illuminating in both. If he had a "supreme vice," it was his perception that good and evil are inextricably mixed. Thus he exhibits a kind of ambivalence which has about it a "terrifying integrity" in that his dichotomy extends to movies he likes as well as those he dislikes.

In his insight into film, Agee became a perfectionist who sought the ideal and was able to explain and demonstrate it. Anyone who wants to create art should thus know his book. A brief, and therefore inadequate, summary of Agee's philosophy is that he represents "the attainment and transcending of realism." His book, actually, is for all readers who enjoy good writing.

1960 A BOOKS - NONE

1960 B SHORTER WRITINGS

1   BEACH, JOSEPH WARREN. Obsessive Images. Edited by William Van O'Connor. Minneapolis: University of Minnesota Press, pp. 190-91, 287, 346.
        Beach refers to Agee as a "wholehearted disciple" of Hart Crane, at least in early poems, and states that Agee felt that the myths of science obscure the "good knowledge" of truth-seekers such as poets and philosophers named in Permit Me Voyage. Agee had the serenity of faith found in

69

1960

other "congenitally Catholic" poets such as Thomas Merton
and Robert Fitzgerald.

2   EVANS, WALKER. "James Agee in 1936." Atlantic, 206 (July),
     74-75.
         Agee did not look the angry intellectual, but had traces
     of gentility and a romantic idealism. He took on the coun-
     try accents of Alabama, yet talked in his own elaborate
     prose style. His clothing was a sleazy cap and seconds,
     which he wore with a diffidence that earned the acceptance
     of the families. They knew why he was there; he regarded
     them as human beings who quite possibly might be immortal.
     He worked in "a rush and a rage," probably without sleep.
     Reprinted: 1974.A2.

1961 A BOOKS - NONE

1961 B SHORTER WRITINGS

1   ANON. "The Rare Legacy of a Poet." Life, 50 (January 27), 96.
         Agee never separated art from life. He wanted to give
     his best and was truly a part of the work he undertook for
     film and magazines. Let Us Now Praise Famous Men is both
     ungainly and compelling; A Death in the Family is great
     despite being unfinished. His film criticism may be the
     only criticism worth reading, and he also achieved mastery
     at comedy in his script for "The Bride Comes to Yellow Sky."
     His attitude was that both the comic and the tragic are
     inescapable in human experience.

2   PHILLIPSON, J. S. "Character, Theme, and Symbol in The Morning
     Watch." Western Humanities Review, 15: 359-67.
         The Morning Watch has an orderly, complex structure of
     symbols and motifs which contrast with the confusion of
     Richard. The work is a study in the maturation of character
     in a sensitive adolescent. The concepts of God and death,
     and the concomitant motif of suffering, are depicted
     through Richard's thoughts and through objects in the set-
     ting. Richard struggles with the artificial and subjective
     aspects of his memory and imagination, achieving a sense of
     reality and objectivity as he realizes his inevitable par-
     ticipation in sin and death. The snake--probably a Christ-
     symbol rather than a phallic image--helps the boy to see
     the nature of human life and the possibility of regenera-
     tion. The work has a rich texture of contrasts, especially
     that of death and rebirth. Death is signified by such
     things as night, the boy's father, flowers, the locust,

hogs, the snake, and the dive. Life is signified by the
coming of morning and of spring, and by the snake and the
dive. Truth comes when Richard is trying least.

3   ROBERTSON, PRISCILLA. "Agee's Special View." Progressive,
     25 (January), 44-45.
          Robertson stayed with tenant families in Arkansas, and
     had a totally different view of their condition than Agee
     did. He was a tragic poet who knew he could not help the
     tenants and trusted no one to help them. Let Us Now Praise
     Famous Men is no more a source book for the thirties than
     King Lear is for early Britain. Through the Southern Tenant
     Farmers Union and the W.P.A., the tenants have helped
     themselves.

4   SIMON, JOHN. "Preacher Turned Practitioner." Midcentury, 17,
     no. 27 (Summer), 18-21.
          In a review of Agee on Film, Vol. II, the writer
     states that reading Agee's screenplays is worth clearing a
     number of hurdles. The screenplays show that Agee would
     have developed into a filmmaker himself. The scenario for
     The African Queen surpasses the C. S. Forester novel on
     which it is based. The Night of the Hunter also surpasses
     the novel from which it originates and is better in Agee's
     text than in the film version ultimately created. A skill-
     ful reader of Agee can remake these films by reading his
     plan for them. Two unfilmed screenplays are the best of
     all: Noa Noa and The Blue Hotel.

1962 A BOOKS - NONE

1962 B SHORTER WRITINGS

1   ANON. "The Unquiet One." Time, 80 (August 3), 60.
          Agee's letters to Father Flye will help to remove the
     mystery which surrounded him in life. They provide both
     a rare picture of a friendship between a priest and a poet,
     and the drama of Agee's struggle to discipline his enormous
     gift for language. It is unfortunate that he never achieved
     such discipline, but the letters reveal his continuing cour-
     age in the battle.

2   BINGHAM, ROBERT. "Short of a Distant Goal." Reporter, 27
     (October 25), 54-58.
          As a Time writer, Agee became a focus for younger staff
     members' hopes and fears. He was thought of as a talent
     deferred, even though he obviously enjoyed his job. His

1962

own foolish fantasy about himself as a writer kept him from
appreciating what he did accomplish. The Morning Watch is
first rate, but A Death in the Family is pathetic rather
than tragic. He should have continued with poetry. His
film criticism, however, is superb; he saw through to the
usually unseen.

3   DUNLEA, WILLIAM. "Agee and the Writer's Vocation." Commonweal,
    76 (September 7), 499-500.
        States that Agee is remembered for what he did not write.
    Letters of James Agee to Father Flye reveal Agee's indepen-
    dence and his anguish over the conflict between his deeply
    Christian roots and his lack of Christian practice in adult-
    hood. He longed for commitment, but was committed to doubt.

4   FITZGERALD, ROBERT, ed. Introduction to The Collected Poems of
    James Agee. Boston: Houghton Mifflin, pp. ix-xii.
        While it is clear that Agee's later poems do not have
    the quality of those in his first book, Permit Me Voyage,
    they do reveal both his ambition and his excellence as a
    writer. The lengthy "John Carter" reveals the Byronic humor
    Agee was capable of. More notable than Agee's masterful use
    of traditional forms is the grand spirit of his early poetry.
    His gifts demanded that he create a prose to carry his elo-
    quent musical structures and his sense of being.

5   FLINT, R. W. "Response to John Updike's 'No Use Talking.'"
    New Republic (August 27), pp. 30-31.
        States that Updike's view of literary criticism is in-
    valid; critics do not esteem slovenliness, as he implied.
    Agee was the Stanley Kauffman of his age, an impressionistic
    critic of film, and a writer whose works can be classified
    as "high-brow populism." A Death in the Family is remark-
    able for its purity of intention. Updike is similar to
    other fiction writers who have erred as critics: D. H.
    Lawrence and Joseph Heller.

6   FULLER, EDMUND. Review of Letters of James Agee to Father
    Flye. New York Times Book Review (July 22), p. 1.
        The letters indicate who and what Agee was. Like other
    exacting, scrupulous people, he tends to undervalue what he
    has accomplished. In his self-doubt and self-accusation he
    seems to represent a kind of American character as well as a
    special time in our history. The final picture is of a
    friendship between a gifted, sensitive writer and a warm,
    kindly, self-effacing priest.

7 HOGAN, WILLIAM. Review of Letters of James Agee to Father
    Flye. San Francisco Chronicle (July 25), p. 35.
       Agee's legendary reputation as a writer and stylist
    makes him almost a symbol of the tormented intellectual of
    the thirties. The collection of letters adds autobiography
    to the myth. It is an essentially unclassifiable record of
    the artist's observation of and response to his own times.

8 MACDONALD, DWIGHT. "James Agee: Some Memories and Letters."
    Encounter, 19, no. 6 (December), 73-84.
       Agee was capable of major work. He had the eye and ear
    of a poet, and showed signs in A Death in the Family of
    achieving a needed objectivity and control. But he was
    too versatile for his age. His relatively early death is
    reminiscent of that of Keats; American writers mature slowly.
    Macdonald corresponded with Agee since 1929, mainly about
    films and writers, and regrets that Agee did not know how
    to "use" Fortune and the other magazines he worked for.

9 _____. "Jim Agee: A Memoir." In his Against the American
    Grain. New York: Random House, pp. 142-66.
       Reprint of 1957.B4 and 1959.B2. Reprinted in 1974.A2.

10 SULLIVAN, RICHARD. Review of Letters of James Agee to Father
    Flye. Chicago Sunday Tribune (August 5), p. 3.
       The letters reveal much about Agee, even though it is
    clear that they have been carefully edited. They are quite
    unself-conscious, showing that they were never intended for
    anyone but Father Flye.

11 UPDIKE, JOHN. "No Use Talking." New Republic, 147
    (August 13), 23-24.
       In a review of Letters of James Agee to Father Flye,
    Updike states that the publication of the letters is due to
    Agee's allegedly "aborted" career, but that this myth has
    grown largely from Agee's own statements of purpose and
    self-accusations. In fact, Agee was well suited to working
    for the Luce publications. His genius was spontaneous com-
    mentary, not patient invention. He should be remembered
    not for his life but for the best of his work: some pages
    of Let Us Now Praise Famous Men, and A Death in the Family.
    Agee's last years working on film were largely happy ones.

1963 A BOOKS

1 BEHAR, JACK. "James Agee: The World of His Work." Ph.D.
    dissertation, Ohio State University, 1963.

1963

        Agee was not really a "victim" of twentieth century mass
culture as Dwight Macdonald and others have argued. He
chose to do his work in the media, and it is possible that
at least one reason for his choice was his own aesthetic.
After Permit Me Voyage, Agee developed a theory that modern
life demands a new kind of serious art using filmic form.
Let Us Now Praise Famous Men was a search for that form,
and A Death in the Family represents Agee's most nearly
successful application of his theory to fiction. His attitude toward popular culture should have important effects
upon academic critics.

1963 B SHORTER WRITINGS

1   DaPONT, DURANT. "James Agee: The Quest for Identity."
      Tennessee Studies in Literature, 8: 25-37.
         Contemporary American writers share the problem of root-
lessness. Agee, despite his use of Knoxville material,
was caught in this identity vacuum. He wasted his genius
on the projects he undertook, giving in to economic neces-
sity. He was beseiged by self-doubt and futility, as his
letters reveal. The pouring of energy and genius into
journalism represents the kind of waste that would have
ensued if Shakespeare had spent his life as a reporter.
In search of a bolster for a frantic, disintegrating life,
he wrote his two final books. Like the typical twentieth
century man of letters, he never did decide what to do and
be.

2   OULAHAN, RICHARD. "A Cult Grew around a Many-Sided Writer."
      Life (November 1), pp. 69-72.
         Agee had many admirers on the Time staff, including
Oulahan. Young writers were drawn to him, and he cared
too much for people--he should have learned to say no.
In addition to his fastidiousness about relationships, he
was devoted to his work and to film.
         Agee's publisher, McDowell-Oblensky, did A Death in the
Family essentially as he left it. In addition to the books,
other Agee material is available in magazines and newly
found chapters and poems. The difficulty in editing Agee
is shown by the fact that Let Us Now Praise Famous Men ex-
isted in a form twice as long as the published version. He
had originally intended to write it for the tenants
themselves.

1964 A BOOKS - NONE

1964 B SHORTER WRITINGS

1   BURGER, NASH K. "A Story to Tell: Agee, Wolfe, Faulkner."
    South Atlantic Quarterly, 63: 32-43.
        Why has there been so much good writing in the South
    since World War I? Its tradition results in individual
    richness. Each of the three writers reacted differently
    to the pull of New York (the Eastern establishment). Agee
    never fully came to terms with life, though in his Southern
    roots he found material and strength for his three books.
    Much of his energy was spent in trying to make order of the
    chaos of the establishment. All that he wrote had moral
    earnestness. Wolfe was more fortunate than Agee in knowing
    who he was, but outside influences hampered him. Faulkner
    never really left the South.
        The three writers used "a grand and urgent rhetorical
    style" nurtured by the South. All three were affected by
    their traditional reading: the Bible and the classics. To
    be a Southern writer seems to mean having a regional, his-
    torical, and universal tone. Burger suggests that Southern
    writers might learn from the experiences of these three men.

2   CHAMBERS, WHITAKER. "Agee," in Cold Friday. Edited by Duncan
    Norton-Taylor. New York: Random House, Inc., pp. 268-71.
        Describes his friendship with Agee, who "'was not reli-
    gious, but about religion.'" Agee was "savagely unconven-
    tional," even "belligerently irresponsible." Reprinted in
    1974.A2.

*3 FROHOCK, W. M. "James Agee, the Question of Wasted Talent,"
    in his The Novel of Violence in America. Second edition.
    Dallas: Southern Methodist University Press, pp. 212-30.
    Reprint of 1958.B2. Cited in 1975.A1.

4   WITHAM, W. TASKER. The Adolescent in the American Novel 1920-
    1960. New York: Frederick Ungar, pp. 118-19.
        The author cites The Morning Watch as one of the few
    American novels of adolescence which show religion as offer-
    ing meaning in life. After Richard's meditation, his spir-
    itual struggles have a catalytic effect on boyish pastimes.

1965 A BOOKS - NONE

1965 B SHORTER WRITINGS

1   FABRE, GENEVIEVE. "A Bibliography of the Works of James Agee."
    Bulletin of Bibliography, 24 (May, August), 145-48, 163-66.

1965

Agee would no doubt resent the myth that has grown up
about his inability to achieve his potential. A full bibliography will begin to give some idea about the quantity
and variety of his works. It is interesting to note that
he reviewed the same films often in the same week for both
Time and Nation, and the shorter Time reviews are often the
more concise and brilliant. Those reviews not listed in
the bibliography can be found in Agee on Film. His work is
divided into the following categories: fiction, drama and
film, articles, and reviews.

2   KRONENBERGER, LOUIS. "A Real Bohemian," in No Whippings, No
     Gold Watches. New York: Little, Brown and Co.,
     pp. 138-42.
          Describes Agee's responsiveness toward life. He had a
     "bohemian" lifestyle in its lack of conformity, but it was
     also without rebellion. He was large and magnetic, with
     just a touch of genius, but his work needed control and
     pruning. His religious nature ran deep, but his willpower
     did not. Reprinted in 1974.A2.

3   MACDONALD, DWIGHT. "On Chaplin, Verdoux and Agee." Esquire,
     63 (April), 18, 24-34.
          Although Monsieur Verdoux was rejected by audiences in
     1947, it was a success in 1964. Perhaps, however, the
     original verdict was the more accurate. Except for Chaplin's
     usual pantomime and slapstick, and the performance of Martha
     Raye, the film is banal and pretentious. Yet critics, espe-
     cially Agee, praise the film for its values, its anti-war
     and anti-capitalistic theme. Agee's explication is more
     artistic than the film itself, and even in his admiration
     he admits the shortcomings of the work. His passionate
     feelings about the theme and about Chaplin dominate the
     tone of his criticism, obscuring his comments about the
     artistic flaws.

1966 A BOOKS

1   OHLIN, PETER H. Agee. New York: Ivan Obolensky, Inc.,
     247 pp.
          Proposes to show that Agee was not a failure, or a vic-
     tim of American culture, but one of the most original tal-
     ents of twentieth century literature. Critics have been
     unresponsive because Agee fit no dogmatic movements, and
     had an unstylish commitment to human reality as holy. His
     poetry, for example, was linked to the English tradition
     and to Whitman and Crane rather than to the political or

anthropological trends in modern poetry. Poetry was Agee's
training ground for prose such as he produced in Let Us Now
Praise Famous Men.

Agee's work on the tenant book was a moral confrontation.
Because of his huge ambition for the work, it is a sign of
his genius that he managed to produce what he did. The uneven reception of the book is due to its character as "an
uncomfortably original" one. It must be read in light of
Agee's stated intention within the work: to create a human
gesture. Its failure to communicate reality whole is, in
fact, part of reality itself. In his desire to break down
the distinction between art and life, Agee resembles modern
action painters. The author's role is to act upon language,
to organize his entire energy toward it.

Let Us Now Praise Famous Men is carefully structured in
a manner similar to a Shakespearian drama or Beethoven's
fifth symphony. Its opening belligerence is designed to
create reality in the reading of it. Then the narrator
becomes quiet, ready to listen and to perceive. The second
major section concerns the essential loneliness of each person, with the condition of the tenants representing the universal human condition. "Colon" prepares for the next
section, an observation of the actual details of the tenants' lives. "Shelter" is the most interesting part of the
book; it can be read as a whole and contains examples of
virtually every technique used throughout. By examining
one actual situation in all of its specificity, Agee in the
role of writer tries to recognize the totality of what it
is to be human. "Intermission" is an angry, frustrated
acknowledgement that literature cannot capture reality.
Using the Mass as format, the next section is a letter to
the farmers, moving from frustration into wonder at the
discovery of a world. The final parts of the work are ex-
planatory in nature, dealing with the need to purify
language.

The tenant book grew out of the Thirties but is a call
to action rather than a propaganda piece. The reader
watches the writer perform an action in response to actuality and is invited to respond with another action. The
work might be described as a prayer, in Buber's sense of
the word; it has the character of revealed truth.

Agee grew up with films. His work with them grew out of
his early concern with photography in Let Us Now Praise
Famous Men. Most reviewers of Agee on Film praise his
contribution to film aesthetics. Representative of his
work in this genre is "Comedy's Greatest Era" (Life,
September 3, 1949). It shows unity of form and purpose
and is a personal response rendered in metaphor that

parallels the style of the film being discussed. It contrasts with analytic, objective criticism, causing people
to become nostalgic for films they have never seen. Agee's
film theory recognized movies as human realities evoking
personal response. As he reviewed war films, for example,
he struggled with the question of his own morality as well
as that of the films. As a writer of scripts, he worked
with an intentional medium which cannot be judged by the
same critical standards applied to media which are complete.
His scripts, on the whole, are less spectacular than many
have believed; but they show his continued faith in the
"real," in detail, in humanity, in poetry.

In the last five years of his life, Agee produced three
fictions of high quality. "A Mother's Tale" differs from
ordinary allegory in that its moral is the resolution of
tension within the story. Its theme is the same as that
of Let Us Now Praise Famous Men, an illogical but necessary
affirmation of life. The two novels of this period constitute some of the best fiction in American literature. Despite the rich variety of the prose, it has consistency of
tone for continuity.

The Morning Watch has a simple, Aristotelian structure
of beginning, middle, and end. Its theme is Richard's
maturing to a realization of suffering and death as part
of human life. Its larger symbolic structures relate to
Agee's entire career. While it does use the American initiation theme, it amplifies the theme of the individual's
isolation which occurs throughout Agee's work. It uses the
religious problem as the parallel of Agee's aesthetic
problem and suggests an acceptance of the limitations of
experience in both religion and art.

A Death in the Family is unfinished. Its basic metaphor
is that of going home. Everything has significance because
it is part of reality. Death, an instance of violated trust
beyond comprehension, does not mature the characters. But
they will wait to see what life, instead, holds. The work
is close to Whitman's ideas; it is not a description but a
realization of reality.

John Updike's comments about Agee are probably the most
accurate. He said that his life was wasted--the way
Blake's, Joyce's, and Melville's were. Even Agee's count-
less hours of talk with friends relate to his artistry;
they are part of an American openness of form. Most American masterpieces are unfinished, pointing toward the
future.

1966 B SHORTER WRITINGS

1   HOLDER, ALAN. "Encounter in Alabama: Agee and the Tenant
    Farmer." Virginia Quarterly Review, 42 (Spring), 189-206.
        In the 1930's, Americans realized that more than 40%
    of all farmers were sharecroppers. Studies focused on the
    effects rather than the causes of tenantry, with cameras
    everywhere to "record" the tenants. Literature so far had
    presented them as a sub-species.
        Agee, full of hostility for himself, his readers, and
    art itself, determined to jar his audience into the truth
    about the tenants. The arrangement of the book, its 31
    uncaptioned photographs and other unusual opening material
    such as a clutter of prefatory and appendix materials, re-
    flects his desire to remove an undesirable buffer between
    audience and experience. Words--not, however, the words of
    one who despises art--became an attempt to put reality on a
    plane with music and poetry.
        Though Agee's love for the tenants did differentiate him
    from his peers, it was ironic that only the educated, such
    as himself, could perceive the beauty of the tenants' lives.
    The reason that they are without guilt is that they live in
    a racial, moral and political vacuum. Their condition is,
    however, the human condition. Action is hopeless and their
    existence is beautiful in itself. Thus the book takes on a
    cosmic tone.
        Agee succeeded in correcting the view of the tenants as
    a Cause. He recreated their individual reality through the
    device of his own and the readers' presence.

2   KAUFMAN, WALLACE. "Our Unacknowledged Poetry." Agenda, 4,
    nos. 3 and 4 (Summer), 68-75.
        By clinging to traditional notions of poetry, we have
    missed seeing the best of our poets: Agee. Let Us Now
    Praise Famous Men is a new vision of the old materials of
    American poetry. It picks up on Wordsworth's failure to
    find the language of ordinary life and succeeds at the task
    of showing the mystery in the ordinary. It is a poetry
    suited to American culture. It is not documentary, since
    Agee did not remain aloof from the material.

3   LAKIN, R. D. "D.W.'S: The Displaced Writer in America."
    Midwest Quarterly, 4: 295-303.
        Criticism and publishing in this country force the writer
    to choose between rebellious or esoteric roles. Writers who
    choose to go their own ways rather than to tailor their
    works for the marketplace suffer from their sense of ir-
    relevancy. Salinger and Agee, however, differ from most

1966

writers of their generation in attempting philosophically based work. Agee is further than Salinger from the main-stream of American values. He concentrates on the subjec-tive, excelling in sensitivity but lacking in social consciousness. A Death in the Family will therefore not prove to be an important picture of its era; it departs from the social awareness of Let Us Now Praise Famous Men.

4   MATTHEWS, T. S. "James Agee--Strange and Wonderful." Saturday Review, 49 (April 16), 22-23.
The writer worked with Agee and was responsible for bringing him to Time as an art critic. He defends various magazines' use of the "semi-domesticated poet" the editors recognized in Agee. Fortune tried to use Let Us Now Praise Famous Men, but it was far too long and virtually impossible to edit. As a reviewer, Agee was easier to edit by cutting; the writer recalls, however, defending Agee when Edmond Wilson attacked his review and judgment of Mary McCarthy, which he had printed in full. Many of Agee's articles for Nation are printed virtually uncut. It is absurd to say that Agee's life was wasted as a journalist. In assignments such as that given him to write the lead story for Time when Japan surrendered, Agee wrote beautifully and morally of the need for a partnership of reason and spirit.

5   ROE, MICHAEL MORRIS, JR. "A Point of Focus in James Agee's A Death in the Family." Twentieth Century Literature, 12 (October), 149-53.
Tension, based thematically in background conflicts of main characters, and structurally in contrast of simple plot elements against profound theme, is the key to A Death in the Family. Rufus' latent personality emerges when death acts as a catalyst on the conflicts represented by Jay, Mary, and other characters. He moves from a subjec-tive to an objective view, the product of opposing forces. Setting, imagery and symbols coordinate in creating a statement of self-realization through roots and generativity.

1967 A BOOKS - NONE

1967 B SHORTER WRITINGS

1   HOFFMAN, FREDERICK J. "James Agee and Flannery O'Connor: The Religious Consciousness," in The Art of Southern Fiction. Edited by Harry T. Moore. Crosscurrents Modern Critiques. Carbondale and Edwardsville: Southern Illinois University

Press. London and Amsterdam: Feffer and Simons, Inc.,
pp. 74-95.
 Flannery O'Connor stated that the South is "haunted" by
the figure of Christ. Agee is a Southern writer who deals
with religious consciousness differently than O'Connor, but
nevertheless is an example of what she meant. He avoids
excess of symbol and metaphor while presenting what
Macdonald called a "moral example of human behavior."
Richard, in The Morning Watch, is in danger of accepting
too literally the images and metaphors of religion that
surround him. He finds that he is moving toward his own,
not Christ's, death and that virtue is hard to practice.
In A Death in the Family, Agee shows the relationship of
religion to a crisis in human experience.
 The second part of the article discusses the religious
figures in the work of Flannery O'Connor.

2   HUSTON, JOHN. "Foreword," in Agee on Film, Vol. II. New York:
  Grosset and Dunlap, pp. ix-x.
 After describing Agee physically, Huston states that his
body's destruction was inevitable. Agee's habits of smok-
ing, drinking, and over-exertion made a constant assault on
it. But he had a unique regard for people's feelings, with
an ability to create community. He did not argue, yet got
people to agree with him by taking their statements and
examining the subtleties until he proved his own points.
Reprinted in 1974.A2.

3   KRAMER, VICTOR A. "James Agee Papers at the University of
  Texas." Library Chronicle of the University of Texas, 8,
  no. 2, 33-36.
 Through study of the unpublished material at the University of Texas Library, scholars will gain important insight
into Agee as a person, a critic, and an artist. The papers,
most dating from after 1946, reveal the methods and inter-
ests of a conscientious, troubled writer who attended to
detail and was devoted to the "dignity of actuality." The
papers can be classified into two large groups: those of
biographical, personal significance, and those related to
literature and to film. Relationships between these two
groups will be of interest, as in the case of a 92-page
draft of a review of Monsieur Verdoux, and a screenplay,
"Scientists and Tramps." Important developments in Agee's
artistry are illustrated by such manuscripts as "1928
Story," showing a disillusionment with poetry, and a
chapter omitted from A Death in the Family, revealing his
intent in the portrayal of Rufus and his father.

1968

1968 A BOOKS

1   CONCANNON, JEANNE M. "The Poetry and Fiction of James Agee."
      Ph.D. dissertation, University of Minnesota.
           Agee's work is essentially the life story of his father.
      He was trying to actualize the future as well as the past
      and the present. His complex life made it difficult to
      attain the wholeness he desired and provided the tension
      for his creativity. His major theme is that of elegiac
      loss, expressing the life-death antimony and other conflict-
      ing elements. His poetry is significant for its relation-
      ship to the prose, but it lacks the necessary objectivity
      and order. In his fiction, Agee experimented with the
      camera and the symphony as structuring devices. Each work
      leads to the next, with A Death in the Family his best.
      The vast autobiography he dreamed of remained unfinished.
      Errors have been made by editors, including Vincent Kramer,
      in placing portions of manuscript within the final work.

2   PERRY, J. DOUGLAS. "James Agee and the American Romantic Tra-
      dition." Ph.D. dissertation, Temple University.
           Agee belongs to the American Romantic tradition. He
      often focused on children, his favorite models were Roman-
      tics, and like them he was concerned with finding an appro-
      priate form to express reality, the ordinary. His Adamic
      figure is always contemplating a lost Eden; his works depict
      death as seen by an innocent. Let Us Now Praise Famous Men
      was an attempt at a Romantic epic, better accomplished in
      A Death in the Family. The tenant book uses the American
      theme that spirit can be discerned in matter, but goes over
      the brink into subjectivity. Though the work can be com-
      pared with Moby Dick, Agee differs from Melville in his in-
      sistence on the actual. A Death in the Family is an epic
      without a bard, subjectivism ordered into an objective sur-
      face. Death is played against his own love and joy in life.
      He is unique in American literature for conveying both the
      guilt and the exuberance of existence.

3   SEIB, KENNETH. James Agee: Promise and Fulfillment. Critical
      Essays in Modern Literature. Pittsburgh: University of
      Pittsburgh Press, 175 pp.
           Agee achieved a unique greatness, applying his genius to
      five genres: poetry, reportage, fiction, film, and film
      criticism. Biographical information, including an analysis
      of Agee's friendship with Father Flye, sheds light on his
      development. Agee recognized that he needed discipline, and
      attained it, working at the height of his powers from 1945-
      1955. He was a total writer, the product rather than the

victim of his times. To say that his commercial work ham-
pered him is untrue; his journalism and script writing were
a natural part of his growth as an artist and a citizen.

Permit Me Voyage is a solid work depicting a spiritual
quest in a world of shifting values. It shows the influ-
ence of Hart Crane and Walt Whitman as well as an Elizabethan
yoking of passion and intellect. The use of a musical structure and the melancholy behind the sensual language are factors which appear in Agee's later work as well. Although
some of Agee's poetry has received the highest critical
praise--"Sunday: Outskirts of Knoxville" is explicated by
Elizabeth Drew in Directions in Modern Poetry--he seems con-
sciously to abandon poetry as a form for his artistry in the
final section of Permit Me Voyage. His desire to re-create
living reality was incompatible with poetry as he understood
it. Words alone, especially words bound by conventional
forms, could only describe, not embody, reality.

If poetry had been "the failure of form," then reportage,
to which Agee naturally turned, was to be "the failure of
reality." It is not impossible to compare Let Us Now Praise
Famous Men with Moby Dick; it, too, is an epic in a grand
rhetoric, a work of paradox, excess and linguistic power.
The complex work was Agee's attempt to create actuality for
the reader, and behind its aesthetic structure it is bitter
social criticism of the liberal mainstream. Unified by its
narrative devices (flashback, chronology, imaginative reconstruction, and central consciousness), musical frame, and
dramatic design, the work nevertheless misses the shaping
hand. Seib believes that Agee was led astray by Naturalism,
an insistence on the absolute beauty of reality. But reality failed to be as beautiful as fiction. Seib disagrees
with statements about the work's moral weakness because of
Agee's attributing only goodness to the tenants; he holds
that this was a deliberate restriction in point of view,
not a moral failure.

Agee discovered that only fiction could give him the
discipline of poetry and the freedom of reportage. Although
he moved from fiction in his constant quest for a form that
would be "a way of seeing," Seib states that Agee's finest
work was done in this form. Though The Morning Watch is a
flawed, sometimes overwritten first novel, it contains
some of his finest writing and most complex symbolism and
suggests the themes of A Death in the Family. The latter
work, a rare affirmation without false vision, concerns
not death but life: family, love, religion, and maturation.
Like Let Us Now Praise Famous Men, the work is shaped by
Agee's love for film, music and drama, but it is a simple,
yet well-crafted novel of maturation comparable in many

1968

ways to <u>Pride and Prejudice</u>. Agee mastered the technique
of balance and antithesis in this work. It is uniquely
American as well as a universal portrayal of human life.
Seib refutes the notion that Agee needed to distance himself from the characters, since his concern creates living
characters.

Agee's move into film work was a natural though not
necessarily deliberate artistic step. There were sociological attractions in this democratic form. It suited
Agee's needs for pictorial representation, yet his best
work was with fictional scripts. He may have pushed film
toward artistic fullness despite the self-consciousness of
his scripts. Seib holds that belittling film as Midcult
obscures its importance; it may well signal an age of
Elizabethan variety and scope. Agee's work as a film critic
was pioneer work, and his body of criticism may parallel
Henry James' <u>The Art of the Novel</u>. His criticism empha-
sized the visual, with honesty and simplicity as standards.
His contributions to the aesthetics of silent comedy are
invaluable.

We are painfully close to Agee for making judgments.
More of his fiction may be found, and books need to be
written about his work in film. <u>A Death in the Family</u> is
perhaps the best novel published in two decades, and it is
a significant change in subject matter for an American
novel. Agee's life was not a failure, but a search for
one medium with the verve of life itself. More of our
writers may take his road, using their genius in new media.

1968 B SHORTER WRITINGS

1   FITZGERALD, ROBERT. "A Memoir," in his edition of <u>The Col-
    lected Short Prose of James Agee</u>. Boston: Houghton
    Mifflin, pp. 3–57.
        The writer describes Agee's life and writing process,
    including the times they spent together at Harvard and
    later. He discusses Agee's attitude toward art and toward
    his journalistic work, concluding that Agee has had an
    effect on prose style. His perceived weaknesses can also
    be taken as strengths. Reprinted in 1974.A2.

2   SOSNOSKI, JAMES J. "Craft and Intention in James Agee's <u>A
    Death in the Family</u>." <u>Journal of General Education</u>, 20,
    no. 3 (October), 170–83.
        Jay Follet's death is presented as a social event which
    reveals the identity of the participants. The book is
    analogous to a film, in which the viewer is drawn into a
    world of symbolic communication. The death takes place

within a larger context, an action within another action--
the writer's rhetorical intention. The accident unifies
the work in the way that the trip to the lighthouse structures Virginia Woolf's To the Lighthouse. The book is a
drama of the mind, arranged like a jazz composition.

1969 A BOOKS

1   BARSON, ALFRED TURNER. "James Agee: A Study of Artistic Con-
     sciousness." Ph.D. dissertation, University of Massachusetts.
         Agee spent his life exploring forms. Three earlier dis-
     sertations have treated Agee from various perspectives:
     Peter Ohlin's is a generic study, Jack Behar's a popular
     arts approach, and Vincent Kramer's an analysis of manu-
     scripts. This study discusses the author in terms of his
     central concern, the mind's reaction to experience. Agee's
     concern with the representation of the "real" in art forms
     resulted in Let Us Now Praise Famous Men, in which reality
     offers a truth and an art above the realm of the imagination.
     After his experience in Alabama and after the atomic bomb
     was dropped, Agee combined his esthetic search with a search
     for the grounds of his own values. Because personal values
     influence perception, reality is dreamlike, as in A Death
     in the Family. Journalism and film writing done by Agee
     were both satisfying and self-destructive.
         Agee's life and work are entwined; his preoccupation
     with individual guilt and responsibility is an odyssey in
     quest of the memory of his father. His subjective reaction
     to perception resulted in a lack of confidence, a mind
     doomed to frustration because of the false expectations
     created by experience. Revised: 1972.A1.

2   KRAMER, VICTOR A. "Agee: A Study of the Poetry, Prose, and
     Unpublished Manuscript." Ph.D. dissertation, University
     of Texas at Austin.
         Agee was concerned with the dignity of actuality, but
     the nature of his vision was a necessarily incomplete view.
     The dissertation discusses material seen as relevant to
     Agee's development as a writer concerned with the individ-
     ual in the modern world. His best work is an attempt to
     give a personal apprehension of minute intersections of
     time and place. From his early poetry, Agee moved to freer
     forms such as that of "Knoxville: Summer 1915," and the
     fusion of subjectivity and objectivity in Let Us Now Praise
     Famous Men. Various unpublished materials show his unhap-
     piness with the world and his search for ways to embody it.
     Notes and variants for The Morning Watch and A Death in the

1969

Family reveal an intention to recreate the particularity of
emotions and to celebrate the physical. Editorial decisions
were generally correct, but there is evidence to suggest
that Agee meant "Dream Sequence" as an introduction to A
Death in the Family. Kramer includes previously unpublished,
edited material as an appendix, including "Dream Sequence,"
"1928 Story," and unused portions of A Death in the Family.
    This dissertation has been the source of a number of
articles, and a book which gives a more detailed treatment
of the development of the writer.
    See 1967.B3, 1971.B2, 1972.B4-B8, 1973.B1, 1974.B2, and
1975.A1.

3   MAYO, CHARLES W. "James Agee: His Literary Life and Work."
     Ph.D. dissertation, George Peabody College for Teachers.
         Biography is important in understanding Agee's human,
     subjective approach to his vocation. Because of the pri-
     vate synthesis he made of the conflicting influences of
     Christianity and Communism, Agee became an exponent of the
     dignity and actuality of the individual. His life gives
     evidence of consistent purpose and unity. His father's
     rural background included distinguished ancestors, and it
     enabled him to attend Saint Andrew's--thus, it was not only
     his mother's influence that set him on the path to Exeter
     and Harvard. A year at Knoxville High School, however,
     gave Agee his final chance to observe the region of his
     birth. At Exeter, he experimented in many genres. After
     Harvard, he experienced the rebellion that resulted in Let
     Us Now Praise Famous Men. Though plagued by his financial
     needs, Agee was faithful to his early commitments, a
     "shadowy saint."

*4   SNYDER, JOHN J. "James Agee: A Study of his Film Criticism."
     Ph.D. dissertation, St. John's University.
         Agee did not express a systematized film esthetic, but
     three major areas of his theory include: the film as a
     valid art form and obstacles to its development; the
     realistic-poetic style appropriate to film; and the
     mechanics of film making. Location shooting, use of sound,
     and use of color were techniques Agee advocated before
     other theorists did so. He was basically impressionistic
     rather than analytic. Source: Dissertation Abstracts
     International, 30 3455A-78A.

1969 B SHORTER WRITINGS

1   CURRY, KENNETH. "The Knoxville of James Agee's A Death in the
     Family." Tennessee Studies in Literature, 14: 1-4.

86

An inquiry into the facts used in creating the Knoxville of the book suggests that the city is depicted in a physically accurate way, and that it is used as a re-enforcement of the themes of anonymity and identity. According to Northrop Frye's definitions in The Anatomy of Criticism, the work is the kind of autobiographical fiction Frye would call a confession. Thus facts and their use are crucial in understanding it.

The Knoxville Journal and Tribune for May 19, 20, and 21, 1916, and the Knoxville City Directory show that Agee gives a factual account of the accident and also of trips taken by the family. By using few outsiders as characters, and by having several scenes take place in a downtown setting, Agee suggests the loneliness of the individual in society. The rural-urban contrasts in the book underscore the basic conflict between Jay and Mary; Rufus buys his cap at Market Square, a place which has ties to the masculine-rural parent. But Jay's life was merged with his wife's; he had become a city person, working in his father-in-law's firm. Agee departs in one significant way from the factual account. Two pastors took part in the funeral service, one a local minister known to him as a child, and one a priest from Chatanooga. In the book, "Father Jackson" alone officiates, cold and distant.

2   HYNES, SAMUEL. "James Agee: Let Us Now Praise Famous Men," in Landmarks of American Writing. Edited by Hennig Cohen. New York: Basic Books, Inc., pp. 328-40.

Agee is one of 32 American writers, from William Bradford to John Fitzgerald Kennedy, discussed in separate chapters. Hynes states that Let Us Now Praise Famous Men has been classified incorrectly. It is a series of approaches to solving a central, insoluble, problem--knowing human actuality. Its attitudes and tone of love are more important than particulars described. Agee used three approaches. Description and personal response complemented one another; the aesthetic approach shows that the book is both anti-art and artful, incapable of being finished. The work may be distinctively American because of its naivete and ambitiousness, but also because it is eccentric and powerful. It might be described as a hymn to actuality.

3   SHEPHERD, ALLEN. "'A Sort of Monstrous Grinding Beauty': Reflections on Character and Theme in James Agee's A Death in the Family." Iowa English Year (Fall), pp. 17-24.

The title phrase is Agee's description of the novel he wanted to write. The writer states that Agee achieved his goal; the book has an exhausting, intricate beauty.

1969

The opening prose poem, "Knoxville: Summer 1915," gives
an overview of the work. Atmosphere and tone, a lyric,
open address to the reader, convey the sense of internal
monologue alternating with direct analysis that comprises
the rest of the novel. Jay is presented through implica-
tion, mourning the loss of self inevitable in the maturity
he also welcomes; Rufus is directly in the process of growth
his father had gone through. Part of his maturation is to
see contrast as a constant theme in life. He will have
identity without alienation.
The Follets constitute a family in a specific time and
place rather than an allegory. Yet their acts signify the
contrast and complexity of reality as Agee perceived it;
their evocative gestures reveal their inner selves, showing
an interdependence between the physical and the spiritual.

1970 A BOOKS

1   REWAK, WILLIAM JOHN. "The Shadow and the Butterfly: James
     Agee's Treatment of Death." Ph.D. dissertation, University
     of Minnesota.
     Death was Agee's theme, portrayed in a range of original
     images in the works which were written from a personal per-
     spective. These include poems, short stories, the three
     books, and Noa Noa. In his early poetry, Agee wrote of the
     fusion of love and death. He moved toward fatalism, using
     the range and the home as the setting for the conflict of
     life versus death. In Let Us Now Praise Famous Men, he
     showed death as a cloud hanging over all citizens, imaging
     mortality through such techniques as the catalogues of
     crushing environmental factors. The book follows a birth-
     to-death progression.
     Agee's subsequent writings mirror his own search for
     meaning in the face of death. Short stories depict the
     inevitable role of death in all human relationships, yet
     indicate that death is a daily process which gives value to
     life. Both of the later books show the possibility of
     growth through a realization of death, but only in A Death
     in the Family does the experience suggested by symbols be-
     come real for the reader as participant. The butterfly
     image has cathartic power because it is well prepared for.
     It suggests that love and strength, Jay's qualities, can
     come again.
     See also 1973.B2.

1   BETTS, LEONIDAS. "The 'Unfathomably Mysterious': <u>Let Us Now</u>
    <u>Praise Famous Men</u>." <u>English Journal</u>, 59, no. 1 (January),
    44-47, 51.
        After a brief history and description of the work, the
    writer states that Agee wanted to lay down an unstated
    theme and present "obscure" variations on that theme. The
    book's center is really the whole problem and nature of
    existence. This is its penultimate thematic subject; the
    ultimate subject relates to Agee's own existence. He was
    trying to "order human cognitions in an apparently futile
    attempt to look squarely into the 'centre' and beyond it
    into the impenetrable enigma of his own individual 'exist-
    ence.'" But Agee found that he had only the power to wor-
    ship the mystery; the question "Who am I?" remained an
    enigma.

2   BROUGHTON, GEORGE and PANTHEA REID. "Agee and Autonomy."
    <u>Southern Humanities Review</u>, 4, no. 2 (September), 101-11.
        Agee's growing reputation during the sixties was tied to
    respect for him as a cultural rebel. The notion of systems
    as a threat to the inner self, a key twentieth-century idea,
    is central to Agee's work. It appears in the film scripts
    as well as in the fiction, poetry, and nonfiction. Agee
    believed that political and economic alienation are probably
    inevitable, but that other threats to the individual such
    as religion, vocation, education, and the family could
    function differently than they do. <u>A Death in the Family</u>
    is critical of the sacrifice of autonomy that occurs when
    the child is taught to trust passively in institutions.
    Authoritarian religion, not faith itself, is Richard's
    enemy in <u>The Morning Watch</u>. Agee felt that individuals
    must be allowed room to make mistakes and also to find "a
    fearless joy in existence." His radical individualism has
    been deplored in his life and ignored in his art.

3   CURRY, KENNETH. "Notes on the Text of James Agee's <u>A Death</u>
    <u>in the Family</u>." <u>PBSA</u>, 64, no. 1 (First Quarter), 84-98.
        Although the editors of <u>A Death in the Family</u> said there
    had been no rewriting from Agee's manuscript, a comparison
    of several pieces from the manuscript published in <u>Harper's</u>
    <u>Bazaar</u> and <u>The New Yorker</u> with the book suggests extensive
    mechanical changes in punctuation and also the addition of
    transitional sentences. The pieces in <u>The New Yorker</u>, pub-
    lished closer to the date of the book than those pieces in
    <u>Harper's Bazaar</u>, suggest the practices used in editing the
    manuscript. One change made after the 1956 publication of

1970

pieces in Harper's was that of the child's name from Richard
to Rufus, probably in order to include a "Rufus" section
Agee may not have intended for the book. Curry provides a
list of corrections needed in the book text.

4 FREEMAN, JAMES A. "Agee's 'Sunday' Meditation." Concerning
   Poetry, 3, no. 2 (Fall), 37-39.
      The author explicates "Sunday: Outskirts of Knoxville,
   Tennessee." The tone of the speaker is subtle and compas-
   sionate, but also certain that work and marriage, money,
   children, and aging will stifle the bliss of the lovers.
   The setting delicately re-enforces the speaker's sadness.
   The poem reverses the time order of most love poetry such
   as The Song of Solomon, looking forward rather than back-
   ward to trials and estrangement.

5 RUOFF, GENE W. "A Death in the Family: Agee's 'Unfinished'
   Novel," in The Fifties: Fiction, Poetry, Drama. Edited
   by Warren French. DeLand, Florida: Everett/Edwards, Inc.,
   pp. 121-32.
      A Death in the Family is unlike other "unfinished" works
   in that it holds whatever real greatness Agee achieved. It
   contains a hidden novel in pp. 11-79, 115-212, and 249-339.
   Other material belongs in the collected prose volume. Editors probably included the italicized material because the
   actual finished manuscript was so unlike Agee's earlier
   work. The main body of the narrative is a representation
   of an action which reveals character. It is rich prose on
   the barest possible frame, showing that Agee had, in effect,
   become his own controlling editor. A new edition of the
   work is needed, because its reputation as "unfinished" is
   unjust.

1971 A BOOKS

1 FLANDERS, MARK WILSON. "The Film Theory of James Agee." Ph.D.
   dissertation, University of Iowa.
      Agee's film theory is implicit in his scattered writings.
   This study examines his normative writings, with some attention to the non-normative as well. Agee was characterized
   by his social consciousness and conviction that the film
   could best express the individuality of the human person.
   Though he thought of art as moral and truth-seeking, he
   abhorred propaganda. He saw danger in the power of the
   film, which those concerned in making and criticizing films
   must take care not to abuse. His theory can be applied to
   acting, directing, writing, and other phases of film making.

The film must show reality as fortuitous, and help the common people to experience an unfolding world. "The Dedication," his script about the world threatened by the bomb,
comes the closest to his own film ideals and ought to be
produced. Several contemporary film makers meet Agee's
criteria, moving from the notion of the well-made play to
depicting man for his own sake.

2   LARSON, ERLING. <u>James Agee</u>. University of Minnesota Pamphlets
     on American Writers, No. 95. Minneapolis: University of
     Minnesota Press, 45 pp.
         Agee's work is characterized by alternative moods of joy
     and despair. His works demonstrate that ambiguity is essen-
     tial, and he preaches this in fiction and in film. Much of
     his work depicts his own struggle as an artist desiring to
     portray truth but conscious of wrong choices. <u>Let Us Now</u>
     <u>Praise Famous Men</u> is a new form, neither art nor report,
     and should be read in the light of Agee's own life and his
     struggle to know himself. His attack on <u>Fortune</u> in the
     tenant book is a sign of the division in his own soul as a
     writer conscious of a superior vision and yet doubting the
     validity of art. <u>A Death in the Family</u> is one of the most
     important things that he wrote. The three novels, read
     chronologically, give his own story. Despite misgivings
     about his film work, Agee critics should realize that he
     did essentially what he wanted to do with his life.

1971 B SHORTER WRITINGS

1   CHESNICK, EUGENE. "The Plot Against Fiction: <u>Let Us Now</u>
     <u>Praise Famous Men</u>." <u>Southern Literary Journal</u> (Fall),
     pp. 48-67.
         Agee's tenant book is a prayer asking the return of in-
     spiration. It reflects his despair at making art out of
     life, and is an example of what can happen when literary
     forms are abandoned. The writer breaks his bond with read-
     ers, concentrating on consciousness itself rather than on
     imaginative narrative. The work shows kinship with Walt
     Whitman rather than the novel. Though the book contains
     much superb writing, its author was working out his own
     identity and identification with others. This process is
     not appropriate to fiction.

2   KRAMER, VICTOR A. "The Manuscript and the Text of James Agee's
     <u>A Death in the Family</u>." <u>PBSA</u>, 65, no. 3, 257-66.
         Article provides a list of errors in the published text
     as compared with the manuscript at the University of Texas
     and describes the variety of editorial decisions made.

1971

Whole portions of the text were omitted to create a consistent narrative tone and style; examples are scenes in
which the Follets debate the purchase of an auto, and Jay
sings to Rufus in the dark. Editors generally chose Agee's
second work in the case of variants, but--possibly weakening
the final text--ignored the variants in a number of cases.
The text should include a list of omissions and variants.

  The manuscript is difficult to read, resulting in such
errors as the use of "settled" for Agee's term "rattled" to
describe freight trains. Some of Kenneth Curry's suggested
errors are not accurate, pointing to the need for further
editing. Agee's variants should be used consistently, mis-
readings of his script corrected, and all typographical
errors adjusted.

  See other Kramer entries, including 1969.A3 and 1975.A1.

3   STRINGHER, BONALDA. "James Agee." Studi Americani, 17:
     211-50.
       Agee has been regarded as a symbol of youthful rebellion,
     a kind of eternal adolescent and mythic culture hero similar
     to James Dean. Most critical essays have been memoirs em-
     phasizing his personal qualities. Several biographical
     coincidences--his appearance in the late thirties when such
     a figure was needed, his contacts with literary personages,
     his personal habits--contributed to the creation of the
     myth. Numbers of American heroes have reflected the avoid-
     ance of adulthood and inability to face reality attributed
     to Agee. In his case, the tendencies to conflict with both
     one's own situation and with Life itself interact and merge.
     His works reflect energy revolting against itself, as did
     his self-destructive life. Introspection mars Let Us Now
     Praise Famous Men, but not Agee's film criticism. In his
     later works, Agee presents heroism as continued struggle
     in the face of life's hopelessness. Death came to image
     this hopeless but admirable struggle. Rebellion is the
     only real virtue, yet endurance is also a cause for respect.

1972 A BOOKS

1   BARSON, ALFRED T. A Way of Seeing: A Critical Study of James
     Agee. University of Massachusetts Press, 216 pp.
       Traces the development of Agee's artistic consciousness.
     His best work--parts of Let Us Now Praise Famous Men and A
     Death in the Family--was done before 1950, and represents
     a tension between his desire to be redeemed through art and
     his knowledge that art is essentially amoral. Much of the
     film work lost that tension, and constituted response to

reality rather than a record of it. Agee's ideas on language were influenced by his work with I. A. Richards and resemble Emerson's. Words, however, seemed ultimately inaccurate. In Let Us Now Praise Famous Men, Agee applied his desire for accurate diction and sensitivity to the ambiguity of language to shape a new way of seeing, an arrangement and production of reality itself. The book belongs more to the future than to the past or present.

Agee was tormented and disillusioned after the use of the atomic bomb, pre-occupied with the loss of individuality he perceived in himself and others. In A Death in the Family, he wanted to depict the betrayal of his father, and went beyond Joyce in merging more than one subjective point of view. Rufus typifies the theme of loneliness and contentment, with the contentment shown to be an illusion. In The Morning Watch, Richard achieves a perversion of rebirth; he has moral sensitivity but cannot distinguish clearly between good and evil. Agee's retreat into film after each significant work represents a succumbing to his lack of conviction about his work. Revised edition of 1969.A1.

2   LAWBAUGH, WILLIAM M. "'Remembrance of Things Past': An analysis of James Agee's Prose Style." Ph.D. dissertation, University of Missouri, Columbia.

Agee used many different prose styles, but he showed a developmental pattern related to his psychological growth and practice of his craft. The factors which affected his style include his father's death, his mother's religiosity, his friendship with Father Flye, his close knowledge of the King James edition of the Bible and of the Book of Common Prayer, his study of classical rhetoric and of Latin, his early imitation of Hemingway, and his desire to merge all of his talents in a style appropriate to depict the real. "Havana Cruise" and "Knoxville, Summer of 1915" are examples of his perfected style, but Let Us Now Praise Famous Men lacks synthesis. It is an example of seventeenth-century anatomy, with its strength in virtuosity rather than in form. Ten years after this book, Agee produced The Morning Watch, his finest achievement. This work uses all of his talents and his personal themes but is carefully formed. Classical schemes and tropes occur throughout. After unproductive years in Hollywood, Agee was returning to his true work and style in the unfinished A Death in the Family, ironically introduced by the early, and excellent, "Knoxville, Summer of 1915."

1972

1972 B SHORTER WRITINGS

1   ANON. "The Perpetual Promise of James Agee." The Times
     Literary Supplement (London) (June 9), pp. 659-60.
          The Collected Poems and The Collected Short Prose, both
     edited by Agee's friend Robert Fitzgerald, are a good,
     solid, but not revolutionary addition to Agee studies.
     Agee's poetry is not important, but the prose volume con-
     tains vital "scraps and shavings." Comparing Agee unfavor-
     ably with F. Scott Fitzgerald, the reviewer states that Agee
     had a huge range of sympathy, but lacked control and needed
     a "saving obtuseness." He seemed to have nothing to learn
     morally, and omitted the usual stages of becoming an artist.
     Agee was really not neurotic enough to write; he was driven
     only by love. With control, he might have been a great
     "positive" artist, filling the need unmet by such writers
     as O'Hara and Cheever. His tendency to compulsive detail
     was the cancerous side of his talent, and although he
     achieved subtlety, he never attained distance. Though
     Dwight Macdonald has praised his capacity for general
     thought, this really blurred his creativity.
          One of Agee's tragedies was his inability to use Holly-
     wood to his advantage, as Faulkner did. He had only one
     mode of creativity--top gear. Thus, one of his key works,
     Night of the Hunter, is virtually unread because it is a
     film script. There and elsewhere, he is a frustrated
     director; his prose re-creates exactly what he has seen.
     Because of his talent and his inability to shape his work
     satisfactorily, one feels both gratitude and regret at any
     Agee reading.

2   BORNSTEIN, GEORGE. "James Agee." The Times Literary
     Supplement (London) (August 18), p. 971.
          Points out an error made by the anonymous reviewer of
     June 9 (See 1972.B1). In The Night of the Hunter, Mitchum's
     knuckles say "love" and "hate," not "good" and "evil."

3   COLES, ROBERT. "James Agee's 'Famous Men' Seen Again."
     Harvard Advocate, 105, no. 4 (February), 42-46.
          Twenty-five years after Agee and Evans had visited the
     Alabama sharecroppers of Let Us Now Praise Famous Men, the
     writer spent the summer in Mississippi, less than a hundred
     miles from the scene of that book. Civil rights workers
     during the early sixties kept Agee's book with them on
     their journeys from Harvard and other intellectual, liberal
     centers. The white farmers who spoke about keeping what
     "belonged" to them as tenants were an ironic contrast to
     the families Agee had written about. At the same time,
     they looked and spoke the way these families must have done.

Much of the pride of the white poor is often seen as a rationalization made in the face of a desperate struggle for survival. Agee had engaged in romantic journalism in his book, omitting the brutishness and racism which were included in the tenants' daily lives. The paradox is that the people do project courage, pride, and spirit, despite their provincialism, which meet the most idealistic expectations of philosophers and theologians.

For the civil rights workers, including the writer, it was easy to identify the black sharecroppers with the beauty and passion of Agee's book, but difficult to associate the white farmers with the goodness suggested by the families Agee knew. The Yankees doubted that Agee could have grown close to or respected the white farmers if he had lived and written at a different period than the thirties. Though they had come to the South to desegregate it, the workers avoided the majority class and race of the region, the poor white people. In long, soul-searching conversations, the Northerners concluded that the oppressors of the blacks were outside the circle of possible friendship--even though Agee's book, for many, was "the" book. Like other fighters, they needed to identify an enemy and stand united against it. A black tenant farmer, however, pointed out that the whites were "in a mess" just as the blacks were, and that if all of the poor would unite, the political system would have to respond to their needs.

The dream of unity has not come true; the races still live side-by-side as strangers, and the poor are still oppressed. Agee continues to remind us of our common humanity, even through the "famous men" of the South.

4   FLYE, FATHER JAMES HAROLD. "An Article of Faith." Harvard
     Advocate, 105, no. 4 (February), 15-17, 24.
          The writer gives background for his and Agee's long friendship, which began in 1919 when Agee was ten years old and continued until his death. The priest and the child found a number of subjects in common, including their interests in fossils, animals, and sports. They also had bonds in "spirit, feelings and instincts." Agee was tenderhearted, incapable of knowingly inflicting pain on others, and humorous without being a tease. The friendship was not a replacement for a father's love, but a relationship they might have had if he had lived. The use of the word "Father" to address the priest was standard at Saint Andrew's.
          Life at the school was not always easy for Agee, since he was absent-minded and often too absorbed in what he was doing to observe the regimen. The school was very different

1972

from the traditional English boarding school, since there
was no system of rank among the boys and they could choose
associates somewhat freely. Many of the boys came from
humble rural backgrounds, and there was a wide ability
range among them. A warm religious atmosphere prevailed,
and included the liturgy of the Anglican Communion. Agee
stayed at the school until he was fourteen, living in the
dormitory while his mother and sister stayed at a cottage
on the school grounds. He began the study of French with
Father Flye, and took his ninth grade class in English
History.

After the Agees returned to Knoxville, Father Flye
visited them occasionally, and he and Agee took a bicycle
trip in France and England during the summer of 1925.
While Agee was at Exeter the two kept in touch through
their letters. From 1941 to 1954 Father Flye took summer
parish duties in New York, during which times they had
frequent visits.

Agee most likely discovered his vocation as a writer
during his first semester at Exeter. His memories of
Knoxville and of Saint Andrew's play a significant part
in his work; the two novellas are largely fact. Though
Agee did not fully accept some of the doctrinal positions
of the Church during his adult life, he retained his
Christian faith and expressed it through reverence and
awe for creation. He had difficulties in making commit-
ments because he could see the flaws of most organizations,
yet he understood the problems with this position. His
great humility and compassion will create closer bonds
among the human family. Reprinted in 1974.A2.

5   KRAMER, VICTOR A. "Agee and Plans for the Criticism of
       Popular Culture." Journal of Popular Culture, 5, no. 4
       (September), 755-66.
           A number of entries in Agee's notes recognize the need
     for analysis of words and images as they are used in every
     day contexts. One entry is an eight-page discussion of a
     proposed new "criticism" which would describe the why and
     the how of cultural values and changes in them. Agee
     planned a series of works by himself and Walker Evans;
     among other strategies, he suggested simply publishing the
     banal comments and dishonest statements of public figures
     without comment in a collection. His own film criticism is
     an example of the analysis he hoped for in all media. He
     believed that the culture fails to reach its potential be-
     cause we lack understanding of it and give way to dehumani-
     zation. One problem with Agee's scheme is that he did not
     deal with the fact that reflective analysis conflicts with

the basically irreflective nature of popular forms. His
ideas, however, might provide impetus to critics now.
McLuhan and others have begun some of the things he wanted
done.
    See 1969.A2 and 1975.A1.

6   _____. "Agee's Let Us Now Praise Famous Men: Image of Tenant
    Life." Mississippi Quarterly, 25:   405-17.
        Other commentaries, such as those of Ohlin, Holder,
    Perry and Seib, emphasize technique and ultimate meaning.
    But the core of the work is the focus on the tenant culture
    itself. The writer, whose presence in the narration makes
    a kind of lyric poem of it, selects material carefully, in
    the light of his own background, to image tenant life.
        An ironic dignity comes from the conjunction of land and
    living. While the book does attack conventional documen-
    taries which overlook this beauty, it also records Agee's
    suffering at the way the culture is caught between an agrar-
    ian and an industrial way of life. Each technique is chosen
    to reflect the particular reality described; Ohlin's comment
    that it is a "book about writing a book about sharecropping"
    removes emphasis from the complexity Agee saw in the tenants'
    life.
        Nature dominates the lives of the sharecroppers, yet it
    allows them to live. Not their isolation from industrial
    society but their contact with it produces their degradation.
    They have become a people unable to make things, savers.
        In the sections on shelter and clothing, Agee uses fac-
    tual techniques to report tenant efforts to stay alive. In
    the education and work sections, he uses imaginative devices
    to set up an expanded image of the reality he wants to re-
    create. From the particulars, both factual and imaginative,
    the readers are to induct universal conclusions about the
    dignified yet victimized culture.
        See also 1975.A1.

7   _____. "Agee's Use of Regional Material in A Death in the
    Family." Appalachian Journal, 1, no. 1 (Autumn), 72-80.
        As early as the 1920's, Agee made use of regional mate-
    rial in his writing. Contrary to assumptions, he spent
    summers and even one high school year in Tennessee after
    leaving Saint Andrew's. Autobiography is a strong element
    in Let Us Now Praise Famous Men as well as in the later
    books.
        Agee longed for what he had missed because of his father's
    death. He saw his father essentially as a victim of prog-
    ress, whose most admirable traits came from his rural roots.
    The difficulty of maintaining continuity in a changing

1972

context, exemplified by the responsibility and frustration
felt by Jay in his family life, is an important theme of A
Death in the Family. Agee's plans for the work included
more scenes with the great-grandmother as part of his depic-
tion of the rural roots. The variant manuscript, reprinted
within the article, contains a long parallel to the scene
in which Jay comforts Rufus. There Jay's mother comforts
him as a little boy, and he remembers especially her youth
and the cabin. A number of scenes in the novel as published demonstrate the city-country conflict, with positive
values linked to the Tennessee countryside.
See other Kramer entries, especially 1969.A3 and 1975.A1.

8   . "The Complete 'Work' Chapter for James Agee's Let Us
Now Praise Famous Men." Texas Quarterly, 15, no. 2
(Summer), 27-48.
Some of the original manuscript of Let Us Now Praise
Famous Men was omitted, undoubtedly for reasons of cost.
The omission of Part I of the "Work" chapter affected the
final form of the book, for it was Agee's intention to have
the reader experience the life of the tenant farmer as
closely as possible. The omitted portion of "Work" portrays
with excruciating exactness the reiterative nature of the
work, in addition to growing and harvesting cotton, which
the tenants must do to stay alive. Families are shown as
economic units, and the reader is given exact directions
for experiencing the patterns of work followed by each
family member. The omitted portion, edited by Kramer, is
given on pp. 31-48.
See also 1969.A3 and 1975.A1.

9   . "James Agee's Unpublished Manuscript and his Emphasis
on Religious Emotion in The Morning Watch." Tennessee
Studies in Literature, 17: 159-64.
Unpublished notes and manuscript suggest that Agee
wanted to evoke the pinnacle of religious fervor. The
story depicts the futility of trying to prolong a doomed
emotion; the frustration of trying to meditate is Agee's
subject. Richard, like Rufus in A Death in the Family,
does not develop. As in Let Us Now Praise Famous Men,
emphasis is placed on the value of a particular moment.
Though Agee had some doubts about the best method to use,
he had a clear sense of the subject of the work. Like the
critics, he questioned the effectiveness of the final symbolism. Use of an omitted introduction and an alternate
ending would have been good for the book. The unused material, reprinted in the article, shows Father Whitman's
parallel attempt to maintain religious fervor.
See also 1969.A3 and 1975.A1.

10   MATTHEWS, T. S.   "Agee at <u>Time</u>."   <u>Harvard Advocate</u>, 105, no. 4,
      25.
          Describes Agee's conscientious revision of a <u>Hamlet</u> re-
      view after the magazine had gone to press, as well as other
      incidents at the office. Not all of the memories are happy
      ones; much about Agee is ambiguous. His complexity tore
      him apart, but made him a significant writer.

11   PERRY, J. DOUGLAS, JR.   "Thematic Counterpoint in <u>A Death in
      the Family</u>: The Function of the Six Extra Scenes." <u>Novel</u>,
      5 (Spring), 234-41.
          Although the editors stated that the book was "a near
      perfect work of art" at Agee's death, this has been dis-
      puted by critics such as Leslie Fiedler. One of the prob-
      lems in editing the manuscript was the placing of the six
      italicized scenes into the narrative account of Jay's death.
      Perry holds that the six scenes, written before the narra-
      tive, are a lens to show the body of the projected, longer
      work: the story of the family without Jay.
          The six scenes are essential in the way that "On the
      Porch" is essential to <u>Let Us Now Praise Famous Men</u>. No
      critic has yet suggested the natural pairing of the scenes
      as the true structuring principal of the work. A contrast-
      ing pattern emerges as the scenes of singing, teasing, and
      protection from life versus encounter are matched. A pos-
      sible new sequence for the scenes could be the placement
      of the singing scenes first, the protection-encounter
      (Catherine's birth and the great-grandmother) scenes last,
      and the teasing scenes surrounded by the cap narrative.
      This would demonstrate the epic nature of the piece, with
      Jay's death seen as affecting the destiny of an entire
      family. Rufus' position is analogous to that of Telemachus
      in <u>The Odyssey</u>.

12   PRESLER, TITUS. "The Poetry of James Agee." <u>Harvard Advocate</u>,
      105, no. 4 (February), 35-37.
          Agee's poetry engages us on a personal level because it
      is concerned with our humanness or driving power without
      being abstract or romantic. He documents conflict, making
      each poem a point of conflict with actual joy or pain.
      There is a strong relationship between Agee's life and his
      poetry, so that the poems cover a number of subjects with
      passionate intensity.
          Most of Agee's poetry was written within seven years of
      his graduation from Harvard. Its chief theme seems to be
      the living history in the consciousness of the individual
      person. The goodness and the limitation of human beings
      are exemplified by that history. While his statement is

1972

spoiled by didacticism in "John Carter," another narrative
experiment, "Ann Garner," more successfully conveys the bond
between life and the imagery which represents it in poetry.
The most exciting side of Agee's poetic vision is the tone
of receptivity, even of celebration, which pervades it.
Without yielding to a romantic tendency to claim mysterious
bonds with nature, the poet shows human bonds with it by
creating metaphors that have a factual, fundamental quality.
He was primarily intent on celebrating love, so that even
in the apparently cynical "Sunday: Outskirts of Knoxville,
Tennessee" he suggests that "this fragile, temporary thing
is perhaps after all the stuff of life." Religion, another
important concern of Agee, appears in the poetry as an en-
dangered value. He rejects the humanization of Christ and
de-emphasis on belief characteristic of contemporary religion. Because he thoroughly accepts the idea of original
sin, Agee's view of the human condition is fundamentally
grim. Life itself cannot be entirely victorious, yet the
hunger we experience for nobility and goodness is our only
means toward human fulfillment. The retreat to love, en-
lightened by awareness of guilt, is Agee's paradigm of a
worthy life.

13   RAMSEY, ROGER. "The Double Structure of The Morning Watch."
     Southern Novelists, 4, no. 3 (Fall), 494-503.
     Agee used a tripartite structure or triptych to give
meaningful form to the sequential narrative. In his 1937
application for a Guggenheim award, he had used the term
"triptych" to apply to photography, but evidence in the
novel suggests that he carried it out in a fictional mode.
The middle section of The Morning Watch, sometimes dismissed
as abstract or dull, is actually two-thirds of the text and
its true focus. Parts I and III "fold into" Part II; the
center of the work is the altarpiece and Richard's movement
toward understanding of the mystery of sin, death, and
resurrection. He moves from immature bedwetting to the
decisive immersion, from the literal to the abstract. The
middle section is actually a paradigm of the childhood and
maturity sections, containing moments of both. The tri-
partite structure gives balance, interdependence of parts,
and harmony in paradox.

14   SAMWAY, PATRICK. "James Agee: A Family Man." Thought, 47,
     no. 184 (September), 29-39.
     The lack of continuity in Agee's writings and the need
for a definitive biography make it difficult to trace a
pattern of development in his career. Though he did not
repeat forms, one theme that appeared in his early poems

persisted in his later writings: his use of family life
and love, especially that of his own experience. Lacking
an articulated film theory, Agee could not integrate his
special theme into his film work, but his literature successfully conveys it in a visual style. The life of one
household becomes the universal human story, with personal
suffering seen as productive. Agee celebrated life, the
heart.

15   SAUDEK, ROBERT. "J. R. Agee '32/A Snapshot Album: 1928-1932."
      Harvard Advocate, 105 (February), 18-22.
          The writer was Agee's roommate during their four years
      at Harvard. He uses anecdotes to illustrate statements
      about Agee's character and personality. Agee was a com-
      passionate person who was not able to cope with the insen-
      sitivity of others. Saudek regarded him as a model or
      wiser, more adult person in many ways--as though his extreme
      conduct were somehow the truly appropriate behavior to which
      the other students were aspiring in maturity. For Agee,
      the best thing about Harvard, which he did not like as well
      as Exeter, was his sense of freedom. He used this freedom
      to experiment with and master styles and forms of written
      English. In some ways, the security he felt with the writ-
      ten word was the only security he ever knew.
          Agee was set apart from others because, while he had a
      deep understanding of human behavior, he feared his own
      actions. His excesses included his temper and his drinking
      habits. Nights were often passed listening, talking, smok-
      ing and drinking; the circle of his friends was wide and
      went beyond the Harvard community, even to fellow workers
      he met on summer jobs. One anecdote, about Agee's concern
      for others, tells of a young man who frequented Harvard
      until he entered a mental institution. Agee, who had lis-
      tened to him and comforted him, felt guilt and sorrow for
      what happened to him.
          Privacy was an important part of Agee's years as an
      undergraduate. After a time spent writing, he would emerge,
      asking his friends to listen to the pieces he had been work-
      ing on. "John Carter" was a poem Saudek recalls Agee re-
      citing after one of his work sessions.
          Other poems and stories included both Agee's desperate
      realization of mortality and his sense of fun and parody.
      A night of celebration after Agee had edited a special
      issue of The Advocate resulted in an arrest and a beating
      from the police which he never fully understood. His last
      act as Class Poet was to recite and read a lengthy Ode at
      Commencement, which he had barely completed in time to have
      it printed on the programs that morning. Agee left Harvard,

1972

hitchhiking to his job at Fortune, with the same simple
luggage and manners he had when he arrived.
In 1971, Saudek visited Knoxville. Agee's old home had
been torn down. In its place stood "The James Agee Apart-
ments," but tenants and even older homeowners in the neigh-
borhood had no clear idea of Agee's identity. Reprinted in
1974.A2.

1973 A BOOKS

1   COLES, ROBERT. Irony in the Mind's Life: Essays on Novels by
     James Agee, Elizabeth Bowen, and George Eliot. Page-Barbour
     Lectures for 1973. Charlotte: University Press of Virginia,
     210 pp.
         After an introductory chapter, "Human Nature in Christian
     and Secular Thought," the writer devotes one chapter to each
     of the three novelists. References to Agee occur frequently
     throughout the book, as well as in the chapter entitled
     "Childhood: James Agee's A Death in the Family."
         Coles states that thinkers and writers ask similar ques-
     tions about human nature--"Why are we the way we are?
     Might we be different?" Citing the influence of Perry
     Miller and William Carlos Williams on his career as a psy-
     choanalyst, he suggests that Rousseau's idea of using the
     novel to teach about human nature is actually a basis for
     his discussion of Agee's book, Bowen's The Death of the
     Heart, and Eliot's Middlemarch. Childhood, adolescence
     and maturity are the respective focal points of the novels,
     with each period treated in a way that dispels stereotypes
     about it and offers a mode of exploring profound philosoph-
     ical questions.
         Agee was not a preacher or rebel, but he gives his moral
     point of view its own reality in concrete situations dis-
     persed throughout the book. Description becomes an enact-
     ment of philosophical and theological issues, as in the
     scene at breakfast where Mary and the children discuss the
     nature of God. The book is more a recreation of place and
     time than an exploration of a child's unconscious or the
     story of Jay's doom, though elements of these themes are
     present. The child becomes aware of change and complexity.
         The characters in the novel are subtle mixtures--Ralph
     almost wins us, Hannah despises Rufus for a minute. The
     cap exemplifies this enactment of the tension between pleas-
     ure and pain, guilt and innocence, good and evil in human
     nature. Jay speculates about the childhood of Adam, as
     would a philosopher or theologian. Children are assigned
     moral responsibility; the boys who mock Rufus are not

"sick" but "sinners." Childhood is an initiation not into deception, as the popular interpretation of the novel has it, but into seeing the truths of existence. Agee's view of the child seems closest to that of Anna Freud--wry, detached, awed and balanced. It is a corrective to the common view, with Rufus seeing what he might have missed had the death not occurred.

2   SILBERBERG, ELLIOT DAVID. "The Celluloid Muse: A Critical Study of James Agee." Ph.D. dissertation, University of Wisconsin.
        Trained in traditional literature, Agee was frustrated by his inability to conquer the new medium of film. His work is a record of a modern search, but it is not a literary canon. From his early years, Agee distrusted high art and searched for new techniques to reach a wide audience. He was unable, however, to abandon writing in favor of film. His admiration for reality was accompanied by a fear of it and a need to escape into art. Let Us Now Praise Famous Men is a record of his struggle to shape life into art; it has a lyric quality because of the interaction of the perceiver with the object. After writing this book, Agee had a style, an esthetic, and a set of values. His film criticism, often praised, is really a crusade and a work of the imagination. His perceptions about the actual medium were rare. He ignored techniques when the moral he sought was missing. The two later novels show his decline. His writing is desperate and confessional, but his artist's conscience remains.

1973 B SHORTER WRITINGS

1   KRAMER, VICTOR A. "A Death in the Family and Agee's Projected Novel." Proof, 3: 139-54.
        Critical debate has surrounded the composite manuscript of A Death in the Family. The decision to place the italicized material between the natural divisions of the narration was that of the editors, not Agee. He seems to have planned a long autobiographical novel of which the sequential material would have been a conclusion. His working notes indicate that he planned many episodes dealing with his relationship with his father. The fragment "Now as awareness" in The Collected Short Prose suggests motivation to remember his past, including persons, in order to express a sense of wonder.
        Though difficulties in editing the manuscript were numerous, some decisions are unfortunate. Misreadings and omission of variants occur. The "Dream Sequence" omitted has a

1973

much different mood from the "Knoxville" piece used as the
preface. It emphasizes that the artist who creates beauty
from early experience gives meaning to the chaos and mystery
of life. Art is seen as having a unique value of its own.
A narrator would however, be limited to what he could
recall.

The notes and the "Dream Sequence" indicate that the
book may have been closer to completion than has been
assumed. The "Dream Sequence" seems to parallel the journey to the corner, a nightmare ending in peace. Inclusion
of this and other variants would give more insight into the
family and childhood remembrances, and more importance to
the factual nature of the memories. Many decisions made
for brevity and coherence may have departed from Agee's
intention. The passage in which Jay sings to Rufus, for
example, is the briefer and probably the earlier of two
passages from which it was chosen. Five pages in which
Mary and Jay discuss the purchase of an auto should be included as a chapter called "Premonition." The variant passages should, at least, be appended to the text.

See 1969.A3 and 1975.A1.

2 REWAK, WILLIAM J., S.J. "James Agee's The Morning Watch:
   Through Darkness to Light." Texas Quarterly, 16, no. 3,
   21-37.

Agee's correspondence with Father Flye, as well as his
journalism and other papers, indicates that in November,
1945, he was pondering the effects of the atomic bomb.
The Morning Watch, written during this period, was his
possibly unconscious search for a solution to the problem
of suffering and death and a return to his roots. While
Let Us Now Praise Famous Men had a chaotic unity, The Morning Watch is really a more mature, formal work.

Most of Agee's work deals with the theme of death. In
The Morning Watch, the deaths of Jesus Christ, Richard's
father, and boyhood yield a new creation, a young man in
control of his own life. In this way, the work prepares
for A Death in the Family, Agee's apotheosis to life. In
Part I, Richard is shown in need of a test of his aspira-
tions. A hint of new life appears as he walks barefoot on
the grass. In Part II, Richard sees that human reality
lies in falling short of goals. This part is less successful than the other sections; it lacks comic relief and
dramatic intensity, but it does represent a growth in self-
understanding. In Part III, despite an overabundance of
symbolism, Agee depicts the protagonist's loss of innocence
and attainment of maturity. Through the death of the snake,
representing Christ (rather than the phallus or Satan),

Richard comes to an understanding of his share in death and
sin. Death is seen as part of nature and of the self, with
the resolution of pain, suffering and doubt in the resurrection. The locust shell acts as a reminder of both the suffering and the victory.

In writing about adolescence, Agee is in the company of
a number of other American novelists. He differs from many
of them in moving from darkness into light, into the possibility of worthy adulthood in a flawed world. Revision and
expansion of material from 1970.A1.

3   STOTT, WILLIAM. <u>Documentary Expression and Thirties America</u>.
     New York: Oxford University Press, pp. 261-314.
     After discussing the literary and social context of the
     thirties documentary, Stott devotes pp. 261-314 to an anal-
     ysis of <u>Let Us Now Praise Famous Men</u>. This work is a clas-
     sic of the form, breaking out of the central rhetoric of
     the thirties documentary. Agee's text is a strain to per-
     ceive truth; consciousness is the true hero. Though the
     form is antidocumentary, it captures the process of docu-
     mentary by imitating the struggle for understanding of
     reality. Agee's thesis is that the world can be improved,
     but must be celebrated as it is. Stott includes a discus-
     sion of Walker Evans' philosophy, as well as photographs
     not published in either edition of <u>Let Us Now Praise Famous</u>
     <u>Men</u>.

<u>1974 A BOOKS</u>

1   LITTLE, MICHAEL VINCENT. "Sacramental Realism in James Agee's
     Major Prose." Ph.D. dissertation, University of Delaware.
     Agee's basic stance toward reality is that there is a
     unity of the physical and the spiritual; common objects
     and actions are signs of inner grace. The "Omega point"
     of Teilhard de Chardin is, for Agee, already here. Employ-
     ing a combination of traditional forms with technical inno-
     vations, Agee depicts the order of the universe in such
     images as the family, religion, and the interaction of love
     and death. The basic narrative pattern of each of Agee's
     three books is the initiation of the major character into
     the order and the mystery expressed by ordinary objects.
     Camera techniques reveal the spiritual essence of daily
     life. No critic has yet emphasized the spiritual basis
     of Agee's work, and to miss it is to miss his meaning. <u>The</u>
     <u>Morning Watch</u>, for example, is a realistic treatment of
     religious experience and the importance of ritual in under-
     standing both life and death. In <u>Let Us Now Praise Famous</u>

1974

    <u>Men</u>, Agee shows that the joy of actuality is independent of
the writer's tortured awareness. The goodness of the tenant
families lies in their combining the physical with the spiritual in the order of daily life.

2   MADDEN, DAVID, ed. <u>Remembering James Agee</u>. Baton Rouge:
    Louisiana State University Press, 162 pp.
        This collection of memoirs and photographs was gathered
by Madden after he attended the October, 1972 dedication of
the James Agee Memorial Library at Saint Andrew's. It includes both newly composed essays and articles printed in
other sources; new essays are those by Madden and by Mia
Fritsch Agee. Both give personal responses to Agee's work
and life. Includes reprints of 1960.B2, 1962.B8, 1964.B2,
1965.B2, 1967.B2, 1968.B1, 1972.B3, B8, and B13.

<u>1974 B SHORTER WRITINGS</u>

1   KRAMER, VICTOR A. "Premonition of Disaster: An Unpublished
    Section for Agee's <u>A Death in the Family</u>." <u>Costerus</u>, 1:
    83-93.
        One section from the 308 pencilled sheets related to the
composite manuscript is a scene in which Jay and Mary
(called Laura in these notes) discuss the question of buy-
ing an automobile. This portion is between a finished and
a rough state. It suggests Agee may not have wanted to
write a conventional novel, but to compile extensive,
eclectic memories. The piece was probably omitted from
the book because it deals only with the parents, not with
Rufus. But Agee may have planned to expand the story of
the marriage rather than the child's viewpoint. The piece
exemplifies the polarity between the husband and wife, and
would have strengthened the death irony. The section is
included in the article, along with Agee's spelling and
variants.
    <u>See</u> 1969.A3 and 1975.A1.

2   STANFORD, DONALD E. "The Poetry of James Agee: The Art of
    Recovery." <u>Southern Review</u>, 10, no. 2, 16-19.
        Agee deserves to be read and remembered for his poetry.
Much of his work represents successful recovery of the
styles and forms of past ages. He also recovered lost
subjects such as love and Christian faith, and made a last-
ing, though small, contribution to love poetry in English.
Many reviewers of <u>Permit Me Voyage</u> overlooked the religious
intent of the poems. Agee could have been a major poet had
he not abandoned poetry.

1975 A BOOKS

1   KRAMER, VICTOR A. <u>James Agee</u>. Edited by Sylvia E. Bowman.
    Twayne's United States Authors Series. Boston: G. K. Hall,
    182 pp.
         Through a detailed analysis of published and unpublished
    writings (excepting the screenplays) Kramer argues that
    Agee had a consistent vision--reverence for actuality--
    which was presented through close observation of the com-
    monplace. His work is an act of perception in which expe-
    rience is recalled and modified by the imagination. On his
    own terms, his career was a happy one. Because he wanted
    to recreate the complexity of ordinary experience, he
    moved to freer forms after <u>Permit Me Voyage</u>. His notes
    reveal that he may have undertaken too many projects as he
    moved into film criticism and film writing, but the mature
    short fiction shares the concerns and biographical base of
    <u>Let Us Now Praise Famous Men</u>. <u>The Morning Watch</u> was Agee's
    first fully successful attempt to recreate a moment; he
    shows Richard's faith at its height. The central section
    which prolongs the doomed emotion is the core of the work.
    Unpublished sections of the manuscript clarify the book's
    design.
         <u>A Death in the Family</u> is more like a poem than a novel,
    depicting death as the negation of life and yet one of its
    necessities. The italicized sections are important, and
    other variants, such as "Dream Sequence," should have been
    included.
         Agee succeeded in documenting what others do not even
    see, took poetry and prose into new forms, and perceived
    the wholeness inherent in modern culture. His morality
    and his aesthetics were unified in a celebration of imme-
    diacy bound by death. Revised and enlarged from 1969.A3.
         <u>See also</u> other Kramer entries for detailed discussions
    of unpublished materials.

1975 B SHORTER WRITINGS

1   MURRAY, EDWARD. "James Agee, 'Amateur Critic,'" in <u>Nine</u>
    <u>American Film Critics: A Study of Theory and Practice</u>.
    New York: Frederick Ungar, pp. 5-23.
         Agee was the first American film critic to be recognized
    as such. His collected writings on film, <u>Agee on Film</u>, are
    comprised mainly of his reviews for <u>The Nation</u>. These are
    serious, witty, and imaginative, the opposite in some re-
    spects of reviews written for <u>Time</u>. Agee's style was to
    comment fully on such elements as action, technique, and
    form, but it would not be correct to call him an analytic

critic. He could be historical and sociological, as in his review of <u>Monsieur Verdoux</u>, but more often he was personal, subjective, impressionistic in style. He often took moral positions, and most of his comments were evaluative.

To understand Agee's criticism, it is important to grasp the key terms <u>realism</u> and <u>poetry</u>. Agee distinguishes between the factual, plain type of "realism," which he endorses only to a point, and "high" realism, which is a form of "high" poetry. This is a combination of surface naturalism and depth of interpretation. Through the skillful use of the camera, metaphors are born in and glorify reality. Most film makers confine their work to a reproduction of objective reality. Hitchcock is a rare exception, since he excels in the use of the subjective camera. Agee's own scripts show that he practiced his own theory, giving different viewpoints in <u>The Bride Comes to Yellow Sky</u> and using color interspersed with black and white to depict Gauguin's loss of sight in <u>Noa Noa</u>.

Agee's use of the term "realism" implies that art conceals art and yet reveals the vital essence in real things. He can thus be called a romantic. His major concern was that a film "interest the eyes"; therefore, he was not fond of the word-dominated films of the thirties and forties. On the whole, he felt that film makers have not fully explored the relationship of image with the spoken word.

Since he was trained in literature, Agee should have excelled as a critic of adaptations. His uneven performance is partly due to his writing for both <u>Time</u> and <u>The Nation</u>. That does not, however, fully explain why he wrote divergent reviews of Olivier's <u>Hamlet</u> for the two magazines. In <u>The Nation</u>, he wrote that filmed Shakespeare could be skilled, but would remain derivative in nature, serving the word rather than the image. In <u>Time</u>, Agee wrote that Olivier had improved on Shakespeare by altering the placement of key scenes. This incident illustrates that Agee's hack work does not meet the standard of "sincerity" he set for film makers in his <u>Nation</u> articles.

Agee's insistence on "sincerity" and "love" in the movies raises an important aesthetic consideration. As Wayne Booth demonstrates in <u>The Rhetoric of Fiction</u>, the moral stand of the artist has an integral presence within a work. Agee himself avoids the question that grows from this situation. He neglects to explain how a film like <u>Open City</u> can be both art and communistic propaganda. The failure to analyze ideas is a shortcoming of Agee's work, as is the fact that he sometimes analyzed only the ideas of films such as <u>Monsieur Verdoux</u> which had a moral tone he liked.

One of Agee's difficulties was that he lacked space to give full critiques of films he liked, but he compensated for this by informing the reader of his personal biases as a reviewer. His humane, catholic taste resulted in numerous wise judgments, such as his recognition that <u>Casablanca</u> was entertainment rather than art. He could write, masterfully. It is unfortunate that he did not live to review Bergman, Fellini, Antonioni, and other later film makers.

1977 A BOOKS

1 MOREAU, GENEVIEVE. <u>The Restless Journey of James Agee</u>. Translated by Miriam Kleiger with the assistance of Morty Schiff. New York: William Morrow, 289 pp.
    Moreau wants to separate Agee's life from legend and help to make his scattered notes available. This is both biography and literary analysis, but not enough time has passed for a definitive biography. His works and his life are interdependent; both reflect the same conflicts. Because of the polarities in Agee's roots, he needed to and did develop a dialectic of reconciliation. Though his notes and other biographical materials show that he often had contrary states of mind, even manic depressions, he moved from anger to love. In the latter part of the thirties, he went from crippling ambivalence into the period of his great work. Alabama was a decisive experience. <u>Let Us Now Praise Famous Men</u> is a search between two poles, anger and the inner life. It reflects disappointment in institutions and a clinging to the values of his earliest years. In <u>The Morning Watch</u> and <u>A Death in the Family</u>, he reconciled the polarities. His film work, especially that after 1950, is less important than the fiction. The legend about Agee probably evolved from his personality and the fact that the writings were scattered.

1977 B SHORTER WRITINGS - NONE

Indices

Index to John Hersey

Williamson, S. T., 1942.B5;
    1943.B10
Wills, Gary, 1975.B2
"Wire-tapping, Nero-style,"
    1972.B1

With the Americans in a Sicilian
    Village," 1944.B8

Y

Young, Robert F., S. J., 1972.B4

Index to James Agee

119